Boeing
720

By Jon Proctor

Great
AIRLINERS
SERIES
Volume Seven

ABOUT THE AUTHOR

Jon Proctor was raised in an aviation family; his father and one brother were career airline pilots. He combined his love of the industry with writing and, in the mid-1970s completed a research project published in 1976 on the Convair 880 and 990 jets for the American Aviation Historical Society.

Following a 27-year career with Trans World Airlines, Jon began writing in earnest and joined World Transport Press as senior editor for *Airliners – The World's Airline Magazine,* later becoming editor-in-chief. As the series editor for the Great Airliners Series, he wrote the first volume, *Convair 880/990,* and is currently preparing a co-authored book on the Lockheed L-1011, Volume Eight in the Great Airliners Series, to be published in June 2002. An avid reader, Jon's hobbies include photography and travel. He was born in Chicago and now resides in Sandpoint, Idaho.

Published by:
World Transport Press
P.O. Box 521238
Miami, Florida 33152-1238

Tel: (305) 447-7163
Fax: (305) 599-1995

ISBN 1-892437-03-1
First Edition: June 2001
Printed and bound in Hong Kong

Series Editor: Jon Proctor

Book and cover design by Randy Wilhelm, Left Field Productions, Sandpoint, Idaho

Digital scanning and film production by Pre-press Color, Coeur d'Alene, Idaho

Press management by The Drawing Board, Burlingame, California

Copy Editor: Billie Jean Plaster

Photo Credits:
Dust jacket and title page: The Boeing Company Archives

The Great Airliners series:
Volume One: Convair 880/990, by Jon Proctor
Volume Two: Douglas DC-8, by Terry Waddington
Volume Three: Boeing 747SP, by Brian Baum
Volume Four: McDonnell Douglas DC-9, by Terry Waddington
Volume Five: Lockheed 188 Electra, by David G. Powers
Volume Six: McDonnell Douglas DC-10, by Terry Waddington
Volume Seven: Boeing 720, by Jon Proctor

TABLE OF CONTENTS

Acknowledgments 4

Introduction 5

Chapter I . . . . Concept and Development 6

Chapter II . . . . Features of the Boeing 720 10

Chapter III . . . . Initial Operators 19

Chapter IV . . . . Secondary Operators 62

Chapter V . . . . Safety 110

APPENDICES

Appendix I . . . . Aircraft Operators 118

Appendix II . . . . Registration Index 120

Appendix III . . . . Production List 123

Appendix IV . . . . Bibliography 128

ACKNOWLEDGMENTS

As the smaller cousin of Boeing's legendary 707, the 720 provides an interesting heritage. Researching the subject has been a fascinating journey for me. However, this book could not have been written without help from many friends and colleagues who share my love of aviation history.

I want to thank all of the people who helped to bring this work to fruition. First, Mike Lombardi and Tom Lubbesmeyer of The Boeing Company Historical Archives provided invaluable assistance and access to that company's vast document and photographic files. At the Museum of Flight in Seattle; Brian Baum, Dennis Parks and Katherine Williams allowed use of the Museum's excellent archival records.

My special thanks to George Anderson, R.E.G. Davies, Alwyn Lloyd, Mike Machat, Howard Martin, Mario Mattarelli, Robert J. Serling, Harold B. Whitman and Bob Woodling for providing important information and materials.

The incredible array of photographs in this book comes from numerous other sources around the world. Major contributions were received from the collections of Erik Bernhard, The Boeing Company Archives, Bruce Drum, Thomas Livesey, the Museum of Flight's Gordon Williams Collection, NASA, Stefano Pagiola, Bryant Petitt Jr., Harry Sievers, Jim Thompson, Terry Waddington and Bob Woodling.

In addition, thanks are due to the following individuals, corporations and collections that have also provided images and data: Airliners Collection, ALPS, AviationTrade, Jean-Luc Altherr, AP/Wide World Photos, Werner Bittner (Lufthansa Archives), Phil Brooks, Nigel P. Chalcraft, Denis Ciaudo, Philippe Collet, Gordon Glattenberg, Eddy Gual, R.J. Hurley, Pete Jary, Marie Keck (Delta Archives), Thomas Kim, Ulrich Klee, Tony Landis, Mel Lawrence, J.A. Morrow, Pratt & Whitney Canada, Al Rodriguez, Nicky Scherrer, H. J. Schröder, Bob Shane, Dean Slaybaugh, Bob Trader, Bob Van Hemert, Nick Veronico and Christian Volpati. For anyone I've overlooked, my sincere apologies; your help is genuinely appreciated.

Randy Wilhelm, of Left Field Productions, and copy editor Billie Jean Plaster did their best to make my work look good, and I thank them for working long hours and meeting short deadlines to get the job done.

Finally, my sincere gratitude is offered to everyone at World Transport Press, for the support and encouragement that helped to make this book a reality.

Jon Proctor
Sandpoint, Idaho

INTRODUCTION

From the first rollout on October 30, 1959, to the last on August 7, 1967, a total of 154 Boeing 720 and 720B aircraft were built for 16 different airlines and the Federal Aviation Agency (FAA). Introduced to the world as the 717 and originally touted by Boeing as a swift, economical and shorter-range member of the 707 family, the versatility of the 720 would grow well beyond the initial concepts. Substantial reductions were made in the weight of the aircraft structure. That and other innovations and improvements would eventually create what Western Airlines would call "the ultimate achievement in jet travel." A clever modification to the wing and the addition of full-span leading-edge flaps gave the 720 exceptional takeoff and field length performance. The availability of fan engines on the 720B provided more power and even better economy.

Airlines in Africa, Asia, South America, Europe, the Middle East and the United States purchased the 720 to provide reliable service on a wide variety of routes in all climates and conditions. The intermediate-range aircraft market was clearly a very important one for Boeing to cultivate with the 720; as an impressive 70% of the 720 customers later accounted for the purchase of several hundred of the company's new 727 tri-jets.

The vast majority of the 720s went on to serve many more years with secondary operators in all corners of the globe. A large number of these aircraft, worn out by years of hard use, were purchased by the U.S. government and parted out for the KC-135 program. Sadly, only a few of these safe and hardworking aircraft remain airworthy today.

The 720 is a tribute to The Boeing Company and its employees who so often seem to come up with the right aircraft at the right time. More than just a shortened version of the 707, the 720 successfully filled an important niche for the airlines and did so with a unique style of its own.

Chapter I
CONCEPT AND DEVELOPMENT

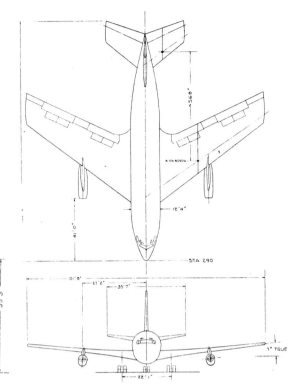

General arrangement drawing of the Boeing model 707-020-6. The study for a twin-engine, short-haul airplane based on the 707 was initiated on March 3, 1956. (The Boeing Company Archives)

On August 5, 1954, just 20 days after the maiden flight of the 367-80, the U.S. Air Force ordered into production the KC-135 tanker/transport, based on the performance of the radical, swept-wing prototype. At that time, Boeing was directed by the U.S. Air Force to devote full attention of its transport division exclusively to the production of these military aircraft. This restriction was lifted about a year later when it was determined that the company could meet its military production schedules and produce commercial airliners as well.

The first aircraft offered was the Boeing 707-120. With a range of more than 3,000 nautical miles, it pioneered domestic, coast-to-coast, one-stop and nonstop trans-Atlantic jet services. The 707-120 flew on December 20, 1957, and entered commercial service with Pan American on October 26, 1958. The second step for Boeing was the development of the larger and more powerful 707-320. About a year behind the -120, the intercontinental-range -320 was truly an overwater airliner. Its initial flight was completed on January 11, 1959, and Pan American inaugurated service with the type on August 26, 1959. With the 707, Boeing firmly established itself as the leading commercial jet manufacturer.

The initial phase of the Boeing jetliner program was well underway with two members of the Boeing "family" in production. Meanwhile, a second phase was already taking shape with concepts drawn up for a shorter-range airliner.

The 707-020

Starting in early 1956, the Boeing Transport Division initiated studies for a new, short-haul jet airliner. Concepts for these derivatives of the 707 were designated the 707-020. The -020 was to utilize the major design components of the 707 with three significantly different, four-engine versions drawn up for consideration. Along with these proposals, four sub-variations – consisting mainly of fuselage length changes, wing span, gross weights, and power plant types – were also studied.

Most interestingly, four variations of a twin-engine aircraft were also pondered. Looking very much like a cross between the Dash-80 and the

737 of the future, plans called for one variant, the 74-passenger 707-020-6, to be equipped with two Pratt & Whitney JT3C-4 engines. Comparing the dimensions of the 707 concept with the familiar Boeing 737-300 puts the substantial size of the proposed twin-jet in perspective. Although the 737 is just slightly longer overall (109 feet, 7 inches, versus 103 feet, 2 inches), the -020 concept had much larger wings. The drawings showed a standard 707 wing trimmed by 29 feet, 8 inches; still leaving a massive 2,100-square-foot wing area – compared to the 737's comparatively meager 1,135 square feet. Even when considering the marginal performance of the early jet power plants, it seems likely that the two Pratt & Whitneys could have provided sufficient thrust for an aircraft with a gross weight of 120,000 pounds. Aside from the twin engines and broad wings, an exceptionally large tail – even by Boeing standards – was the proposal's most distinctive attribute.

Since customer interest for a short-range, pure-jet transport was just beginning to emerge, Boeing's primary focus for the next 16 months remained on bringing the 707-120 Jet *Stratoliner* and the 707-320 *Intercontinental* to market. Meanwhile, the manufacturer continued to refine its design studies and stress to 707 customers the advantages of a similar airliner for short-to-medium routes.

The 717

In July 1957, with more than 150 orders for the 707 on the books and the first production aircraft moving down the assembly line, the Boeing Airplane Company formally announced plans for its next jet transport. Conceived as an economical, short-range 707, the Boeing 717 turbojet was designed to carry 88 to 130 passengers on routes from 200 to 1,700 miles. With many airlines interested in adding the speed and prestige of pure-jet aircraft on shorter segments, Boeing's leaders felt the 717 provided several advantages over propeller-driven aircraft. These benefits included an attractive purchase price, excellent fuel economy, the ability to operate out of airports currently served by propliners, increased passenger comfort and a cruising speed over 150 miles per hour faster than any existing aircraft.

The Boeing Airplane Company presented a detailed look at plans for its new 717 in August 1957. The general size and shape of this concept provided a good indication of what the final version of the 720 would look like. Note that the aircraft is equipped with a short vertical stabilizer and high-frequency-probe antenna. (Courtesy of Howard Martin)

Initially, all of the external dimensions of the 717 and the 707-120 were to be identical, with maximum gross weight being the primary difference between the aircraft (185,000 pounds, versus the 707-120's 247,000 pounds). Planned reduction in range and payload allowed Boeing to design a significantly lighter structure and decrease the fuel capacity to 10,092 gallons. To achieve this reduction in weight, structural items such as the gauge of the skin were to be made thinner, and lighter-weight forgings were planned for the landing gear.

The 717 offered the ability to utilize then-existing runways at airports around the world. Boeing stated that a modest field length of 5,400 feet

was necessary for takeoff at full gross weight, with landings requiring just 100 additional feet. Power from four Pratt & Whitney advanced JT3 engines would produce sufficient thrust for a cruising speed between 550 and 600 mph. Plans called for other power plants in the 10,000-pound-thrust class, such as the General Electric J79, to be made available at the customer's request. These dry-rated engines also saved substantial weight.

After the 707-120 and -320, the 717 was designated to be the third member in a growing series, or "family" of jet airliners. Boeing intended the 717 to be built on the same production lines, with the same jigs and tooling as the 707. Commonality of major components between the

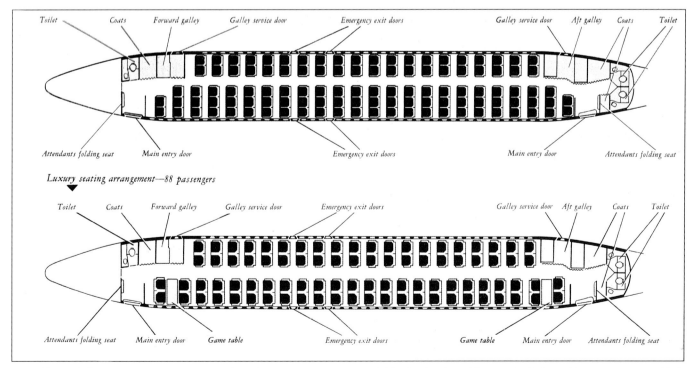

Two different 717 seating arrangements were shown by Boeing in the August 1957 sales brochure. The standard (all-coach) arrangement provided a five-abreast, 110-passenger configuration. The brochure also featured a luxury first-class plan for 88 passengers. This concept also showed four over-wing emergency exits on the 717. (Courtesy of Howard Martin)

models was also planned from the start. The cockpits were identical, the same ground handling equipment could be used throughout an all-Boeing fleet and common spare parts between the three jets eased supply and logistical problems. Interior furnishings such as seats, passenger service units, galleys, carpets, and wall panels were all to be interchangeable. Boeing touted this similarity in features and its corresponding economy when airline managers were looking to purchase a range of jet aircraft for their fleets.

Plans were made to phase in 717 construction with the existing 707 production by mid-1960. Boeing planners saw great potential for their new airliner. With hundreds of propeller-driven airliners made seemingly obsolete overnight by the Jet Age, the future success of the 717 seemed well assured.

Decision to Proceed

The Boeing News Bureau announced plans to produce the Boeing 720, "an advanced type short- to medium-range jet transport," on November 19, 1957. The 720 replaced the previously announced model 717 that found no buyers during the latter half of 1957. Boeing management had clearly done its homework over the summer, working with customers and suppliers to make numerous improvements in the 717 design. Three days later, United became the launch customer by ordering 11 of the new jets.

The United Air Lines Factor

United Air Lines entered the Jet Age under the leadership of its president, William A. "Pat" Patterson. Impressed by the performance of Boeing's pure-jet prototype – but wary of the fuselage he felt was too narrow – Patterson chose not to purchase the 707 after he was told the cabin could only be made longer, not wider. Douglas had agreed to provide a jet aircraft of similar size, range and speed that was wide enough for six-abreast seating. Its reward for building such an aircraft was a $175-million contract for 30 of the DC-8 jetliners from United. The loss of this large order to Douglas provided a wake-up call for Boeing's design team, which later found that it could actually widen the 707s fuselage after all.

United was also in the market for a new aircraft for its shorter routes. The Lockheed Electra turboprop was a serious contender and the airline was close to negotiating a deal for the aircraft when the decision was made to wait for, as Patterson said, "the right airplane." To meet growing

customer demand, this meant the new aircraft must be powered by pure-jet engines. For intermediate routes such as San Francisco to Chicago or Seattle to Los Angeles, the need still remained, and Convair had the edge with plans for its speedy 880.

Once again, it seemed to take the loss of a major order to bring the point home for Boeing. Delta and TWA had ordered 40 of the 880s, and now United was also on the verge of going with Convair for as many as 30 jets. "The sale of the 880 to TWA crystallized our decision here," a Boeing official stated. "It was either go ahead with the 720 or risk losing the domestic operators to Convair." In anticipation of a United order, the champagne was virtually on ice at Convair headquarters in San Diego, and an article in *Aviation Week* magazine announced, "United Wants 880s." However, a wider cabin with six-abreast seating, standardized engine maintenance with the DC-8 and a per-plane price about $200,000 less than the 880 sealed the deal for Boeing. Patterson's decision to purchase the short- to medium-range 720 was a major step in establishing the Seattle company as the undisputed leader in that market.

Why Seven-Twenty?

So what happened to the 707-020 and the 717? United's Patterson was again instrumental in shaping the history of the third Boeing jetliner. He was concerned with the image of his airline going back to Boeing to order 707s after it had invested so heavily in the Douglas DC-8, especially when the smaller 707 was designated with the less significant model number "020." It appears that he wanted a different designation to avoid the appearance of having second thoughts about the DC-8 order, and he urged Boeing to come up with a new identity for its jet. Anxious to land the launch customer for its mid-range airliner, Boeing agreed. The sound of "Seven-One-Seven" or "Seven-Seventeen" also held little appeal to Patterson, and it too was rejected. After some consideration, United's new airliner became the Boeing "Seven-Twenty."

Managers of most airlines ordering the aircraft seemed to be pleased with the designation, and all but three carried "Boeing 720" fuselage titles. The most notable exception was United's arch rival American Airlines, which referred to its 720s as "707 Jet Flagships," and the 720Bs as "707 Astrojets." TWA's four leased 720B aircraft carried the name "SuperJet," but not the model number. The three Aer Lingus jets just carried "Boeing" titles without specifying the type.

BOEING 707-020 SHORT-RANGE JET CONCEPTS

Version	707-020-1	-2, 3, 4, 9	-5, 6	-7	-8	-10
Engines	Four	Four	Two	Two	Two	Four
Seating Capacity	85	87	74	*	*	87
Dimensions:						
Wing Area (sq. ft.)	2,433	2,433	2,100	2,100	2,100	2,322
Wingspan	130 ft 10 in	130 ft 10 in	101 ft 8 in	101 ft 8 in	101 ft 8 in	120 ft
Tail Height	38 ft 3 in	38 ft 1 in	35 ft 3 in	35 ft 3 in	35 ft 3 in	38 ft 1 in
Body Length	115 ft 6 in	108 ft 10 in	97 ft 2 in	100 ft 6 in	109 ft 10 in	108 ft 10 in
Overall Length	121 ft 2 in	114 ft 6 in	103 ft 8 in	106 ft 2 in	115 ft 6 in	114 ft 6 in
Weights (pounds):						
Empty Operating	89,840	81,360**	69,620	*	*	91,210
Gross Takeoff	160,000	140,000	120,000	*	*	160,000
Powerplant	RR Avon 29	P&W JT8A-1	RR Avon (-5) P&W JT3C (-6)	P&W J-75	RR Conway	P&W J-57

* Not stated in Boeing documentation
** Differences in types 2, 3, 4, and 9 were primarily variations in gross weight.

The Competition: Convair's 880

With its graceful lines, the Convair 880 certainly merits consideration as one of the most beautiful jet airliners ever built. Until the debut of the Boeing 727, the 880 provided the 720 with its only serious competition in the short- to medium-range pure-jet market. (General Dynamics Corporation)

After Boeing and Douglas, Convair became the third American manufacturer to produce a commercial jet transport. Development of the 880 began in September 1956, on the basis of the orders from Delta and TWA. Prior to production, the aircraft received the designations *Skylark, Golden Arrow,* 600 (as in miles per hour), and finally the 880 (referring to feet per second). A comprehensive study by Convair had determined that the greatest need of the airlines was for a smaller-capacity, high-performance jet for the domestic market to complement the larger, long-range 707 and DC-8. The graceful aerodynamic lines that provided the 880 with its outstanding speed also led to its downfall. The form of the aircraft restricted the width of the cabin to five-abreast seating and a maximum passenger capacity of 120. The 720, especially with the fan-engine "B" model, was able to either meet or exceed the performance of the Convair, while carrying larger payloads at lower costs.

720—
880—

The 880 made its maiden flight exactly 300 days ahead of the 720. The Convair jetliner was also first to enter airliner service, starting with Delta on May 15, 1960, versus July 5 for the 720. Following the two initial sales, orders were slow in coming and United's abrupt change from an anticipated 30 aircraft to zero was a severe blow to the program. A grand total of 65 Convair 880s were built, coincidentally identical in number to the production of the turbine-powered 720. The Convair airliner program completed a total of 102 aircraft (both 880 and 990 series) and lost parent company General Dynamics more than $400 million.

This cross-section shows the differences in cabin width between the de Havilland Comet IV, Convair 880 and Boeing 720. The importance of Boeing's decision to widen the fuselage of the 707 is apparent when compared to the aircraft of the competition. (Museum of Flight Archives)

Chapter II
FEATURES OF THE BOEING 720

Evolution complete, this 1960 cutaway view pictures the 720 as it was marketed to the airlines. (The Boeing Company Archives)

Although the design of the 720 was generally the same aircraft as the 717, it continued to evolve even after the initial orders were announced. The size of the airliner wasn't firmly determined until well into 1958. Initial published reports on the 717 stated it "will to have the same external dimensions as the 707-120 Jet Stratoliner (144 feet, 6 inches)." *Aviation Week*, in announcing the new "707-720" version, proclaimed it was "similar in size to the 707-80 prototype (127 feet, 10 inches)." Donald W. Finlay, chief of preliminary design for the Boeing Airplane Company Transport Division, reported on January 8, 1958 that "the 720 is identical with the 707s ordered by QANTAS Empire Airways, Ltd. (134 feet, 6 inches)." The length of the 720 that finally went into production was actually set at 136 feet, 2 inches.

In addition to the modifications already announced upon introduction of the 717, a number of new and unique features were incorporated into the 720, making it possible to meet the performance levels that the company had guaranteed. Weight reduction was a primary concern, so the proposed methods for lightening the 717 (reduced-weight forgings, thinner skins and structures, and lighter-weight engines) were put into actual production.

The Wing

Perhaps the most distinctive element of the 720 was its highly efficient wing. The standard 707-120 wing was modified with a refinement of the leading edge to increase the angle of sweepback and decrease the wing thickness ratio. Simply speaking, without changing the basic structure of the wing itself, a fiberglass attachment was placed between the fuselage and the inboard engines. This addition changed the contour of the wing, moving the leading edge in this area forward. Known as the "glove," it offered an increase in the cruising speed (by more than 14 miles per hour) and improved the 720s takeoff and landing performance.

Another feature of the 720 wing was the installation of "full-span" leading-edge flaps. These were designed to extend automatically and in

The unique "double taper" of the leading edge is depicted clearly in this photograph of American Airlines N7527A (msn 18013). The entire upper surface of the "glove" is shown extending from the inboard engine strut to the fuselage. The forward row of 23 vortex generators stands on top of the wing, directly behind the inboard engine. The leading-edge flaps are also extended. (The Boeing Company Archives)

An important innovation incorporated on the 720 was the full-span, leading-edge flaps that worked in conjunction with the main flaps. Shown here fully extended on N7201U (msn 17907), the leading-edge devices increased lift during takeoff and landing. (The Boeing Company Archives)

Viewed from behind the wing, the control surfaces of the 720 are shown fully extended. Below the wing, from left to right, are the fillet and inboard and outboard flaps. Above the wing and on the trailing edge are the inboard spoiler, inboard aileron, outboard spoiler and the outboard aileron. Balance tabs can be seen on the ailerons. (The Boeing Company Archives)

synchronization with the trailing-edge wing flaps. The effect increased lift at high angles of attack during takeoff, climbout, approach and landing. The additional lift produced by the leading-edge flaps allowed the 720 to land and take off at speeds lowered by as much as 7 to 11 miles per hour, depending on the gross weight.

The Tale of the Tail

Three types of vertical stabilizers were installed on 720/720B aircraft. First off the assembly line was United's short tail 720 without the high-frequency (HF) probe antenna or ventral fin. Standing just over 38 feet high, this variant appeared briefly on the first two United Air Lines 720s (N7201U and N7202U, msn 17907 and 17908). Before delivery, the tails of

these two aircraft were extended 40 inches (still without HF antennas). Small ventral fins and full-range, boosted rudders were also installed. These additions improved low speed flight handling characteristics and directional stability, and eliminated rudder "float."

The updated, 41-feet, 7-inch tall, vertical stabilizers and small ventral fins also appeared on the remaining 27 United 720s as well as the 25 American Airlines 720s and 720Bs. The 15 other original delivery customers selected the taller tail with HF antenna and small ventral fin.

Engines

Pratt & Whitney played a significant role in the success of the new airliner by developing the JT3C engine. Two versions of the turbojet

The two main variations of the 720/720B "tall" vertical stabilizer are shown. United Air Lines' fleet of 29 720-022s did not carry the popular high frequency (HF) probe antenna. Compare the distance from the top of the rudder to the top of the fin on the 720 with the same area on the "short tail" 367-80 in the background. The traditional 707 look of the HF antenna is carried on Pacific Northern Airlines' N720V (msn 18376). The first El Al 720B, 4X-ABA (msn 18424), can be seen in the background. An early style ventral fin was installed on the United jet, with the standard model shown on the PNA 720. Also note the lack of static wicks on the trailing edges of the United jet. (The Boeing Company Archives)

were produced for the 720, with 16 of the 17 initial customers choosing the JT3C-7. The -7 version produced 12,000 pounds of dry takeoff thrust and, weighing just 3,495 pounds, provided the required performance without a need for water injection. Besides a substantial savings in weight, the plumes of thick, black smoke typical of jet aircraft taking off while using water injection were gone. Only Eastern Air Lines chose to exchange a 55-pound per engine penalty for an additional 1,000 pounds of dry thrust, by selecting the JT3C-12. Despite other engines on the market, Pratt & Whitney remained the exclusive engine supplier for the entire 720/720B production.

Each of the four engines was enclosed in strut-mounted nacelles suspended below and forward of the wing leading edge. Thrust reversers and sound suppressors were incorporated into each engine tail cone. To provide self-sufficient starting, each engine was equipped with a pneumatic starter, and each inboard engine had an inline combustion starter.

Door to the Future

An important feature in the development of the 707 and the 720 was the outward-opening, plug-type door, a successful concept still in use today. A unique feature of the door Boeing designed was that it was both higher and wider than its doorway. When the handle was rotated, cams and linkages were moved to unlatch the door and fold the upper and lower ends to reduce its height. This action allowed the door to be pushed edgewise through the opening. Closed, it was forced against the doorway by the action of the locking mechanism and sealed by cabin air pressure. Before being approved for use on board the aircraft, Boeing opened

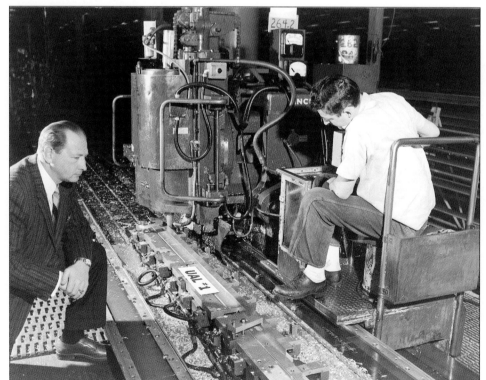

Initial 720 construction began when the first metal was cut on February 4, 1959. Mr. A.L. Salmon (left) supervises the work done by Thomas Stevens. (The Boeing Company Archives)

Brilliant in its United colors and Boeing 720 titles, the first 720 (msn 17907) makes its public debut on the preflight apron at the Renton factory. (The Boeing Company Archives)

and closed the door approximately 25,000 times during its development. The door was also tested for air and water leakage, and its ability to be opened in icy conditions. In its sales documentation, Boeing pointed out that "large as it is, the door can be operated with ease by the most petite stewardess."

Assembly and Rollout

Tooling for the expanding production of the 707-320 and 720 sub-assemblies was installed in Bay 4 of the expansive Plant 2 at Boeing Field. Plant 2 had been primarily used for the wartime assembly of the famous B-17 *Flying Fortress*, then the 377 *Stratocruiser*, and initial B-47 and B-52 construction. The growing need for 707/720 parts required the consolidation of B-52 final assembly work to a single-line system elsewhere in the plant.

The assembly process began as soon as the first metal was cut. The 720 was phased into the regular 707 production sequence at the Boeing Airplane Company's Transport Division factory in Renton, Washington. Because of the similarities between types, the many versions of the 707, the military C- and KC-135 and the 720 all moved down the same production line. A good example of just how

complicated this process could get was when, at one point in December 1961, there were 17 aircraft on the line in various stages of completion, in 11 different configurations.

A look at line numbers, which signify production sequence, shows the variety of types that were produced simultaneously. Line numbers 199 to 201 included, in order, such diverse types as an American 720-023B (msn 18032), an Air India 707-437 (msn 18055), and a QANTAS 707-138B (msn 18067). All three of these aircraft were completed and made maiden flights within nine days of each other. So despite the complexities of assembling numerous types of aircraft, the 720 began and remained on schedule throughout the life of the 154-aircraft program.

A total of 209 days elapsed from the first metal cut to the rollout of the number one aircraft.

First Flight and Certification Testing

The maiden flight of the Boeing 720 took place from the Renton Municipal Airport on November 23, 1959. At the controls were two of Boeing's best test pilots, A.M. "Tex" Johnston and S.L. "Lew" Wallick. As chief test pilot, Johnston had flown a number of "firsts" for Boeing, including the YB-52, 367-80, KC-135, 707-120 and -320. Wallick also piloted several first

Departing into the typically cloudy skies of the Pacific Northwest, the first flight of the Boeing 720 (N7201U/msn 17907) took place on Monday, November 23, 1959. (The Boeing Company Archives)

Identified by the large "billboard" lettering proclaiming the identity of the first of a new type of aircraft, msn 17907 undergoes final assembly just prior to rollout. (The Boeing Company Archives)

The production cycle neared the end at the final assembly "horseshoe." Leading the pack is an American 720B, identifiable by the colorful, orange ailerons. (The Boeing Company Archives)

After little more than an hour, Tex Johnston and Lew Wallick completed the initial flight with a flawless landing at Boeing Field. The new airliner performed all planned tests perfectly during the flight. (The Boeing Company Archives)

flights during his long career with Boeing, such as the XB-47D, 707-320 (again with Tex), 727-100 and -200, 737-100, 747SP, 767 and 757.

The handling qualities and performance of the 720 became immediately apparent during the initial flight. A series of tests were performed satisfactorily and after just over an hour of uneventful flying, N7201U landed at Boeing Field.

After the numerous shakedown flights, the FAA certification process began on January 18, 1960, with two 720s initially involved. N7202U (msn 17908) had been assigned after making its first flight on January 8. A third aircraft, N7203U (msn 17909), joined the test program in March. Because of the experience gained with the 707, government approval for the 720 was expected in a relatively short time.

In addition to general airworthiness, a number of performance aspects were examined during these tests, including maximum-gross-weight takeoffs and landings, stalls, control characteristics and flight flutter investigation. Speeds up to Mach 0.95 (in excess of 650 miles per hour) were accomplished on the first high-speed flight.

A dramatic demonstration of the 720's short-field characteristics was performed to illustrate its ability to operate from limited-length runways. Simulating a steep landing approach over a 50-foot obstacle,

the aircraft, with a gross weight 135,000 pounds, came to a full stop within 2,200 feet after making contact with the runway, in spite of a 6-mile-per-hour tailwind.

As the program passed the halfway point, a 720 was flown to Edwards Air Force Base in California for refused takeoff tests. Fourteen of these punishing demonstrations were performed to determine the emergency-braking capabilities of the aircraft. Accelerated to a "go/no-go" speed of 165 miles per hour, the engines were throttled back and brakes were applied to stop the speeding aircraft in the shortest possible distance. Two of the runs were made at 230,000 pounds, 13,000 pounds above the maximum gross weight. In spite of the extra weight and loads imposed on the brakes, the 720 completed all of the runs without blowing a single tire.

Final tests fitted plastic "ice" on the leading edges of the wings and on the leading edge flaps to demonstrate stability and control under icing conditions.

After five months, the three 720s had flown a total of 442 hours (148 of these hours specifically related to FAA certification), and completed all certification testing. The process culminated with receipt of the Federal Aviation Administration (FAA) Number 4A28 Type Certificate on June 30, 1960, approving the 720 for scheduled airline service.

The second 720 off the line shines in its brand-new United Air Lines livery. N7202U (msn 17908) is tugged back from the paint hangar at Renton shortly before its first flight. Note the size of the original vertical stabilizer, which would be enlarged by an additional 40 inches prior to delivery. (The Boeing Company Archives)

N7202U (msn 17908) arrives at a very soggy Boeing Field after a test flight. The first 720 painted in full United colors, it was the second of three aircraft enlisted for use in the FAA certification program. (The Boeing Company Archives)

The 720B

On August 20, 1959, Boeing officially introduced the two newest members of its growing family. The 707-120B and the 720B were developed with the Pratt & Whitney JT3D turbofan engine. The performance advantage of the fan engine over the turbine was substantial: a 41% increase in available thrust with less than a 20% increase in gross weight, improving the already outstanding performance of the Boeing 720.

A turbofan is simply a turbojet with a large-diameter compressor added to the front end of the engine. This fan compresses air fed into the engine for combustion as well as blowing some of that air outside of the engine. The cold air ducted outside of the engine cowling accounts for nearly half of the thrust of the B-model engine. Driven by a turbine at the rear of the engine, the fan engine provided a substantial increase in thrust, fuel economy and reduced noise generated by the engine. It also created more thrust at lower speeds, allowing operations at airports too small for even the standard 720.

The addition of the turbofan was the only major change in the 720B. However, the 707-120B received some of the design improvements that were originally incorporated and proven in use on the 720. The revised, inboard wing leading edge – or "glove" – and full-span, leading-edge flaps were added to the 707-120B.

American Airlines had earlier announced that it would convert its entire fleet of 50 Boeing jetliners, in service and on order, to the "B" version as soon as the engines were made available. Of the 25 720-023s ordered by American, 10 were delivered with the original turbine engines and the remaining 15 ordered with fans. A total of 89 out of 154 aircraft built were ordered as 720Bs.

Pratt & Whitney JT3 Turbojet and Turbofan Comparison		
	JT3C-7	**JT3D-1**
Diameter (inches)	38.9	53.0
Length (inches)	136.8	136.6
Frontal area (sq. feet)	8.2	15.3
Weight (pounds)	3,495	4,170
Takeoff thrust (pounds)	12,000	17,000
Cruise thrust (pounds)	9,500	13,800

Ferried to Edwards Air Force Base, the first 720B was subjected to a series of endurance tests to determine brake capacity and performance during takeoffs and landings. Shown here between flights, N7537A (msn 18023) carried full American colors as well as Boeing test markings. (The Boeing Company Archives)

Certification

The process of certification for the 720B proceeded quickly after the first 720B (msn 18023) made a 2-hour, 56-minute initial flight on October 6, 1960. The new aircraft continued its development and demonstration flying, with some 60 hours logged in preparation for the FAA testing that began in mid-December. Once the certification program began, the aircraft was sent around North America for an intense series of tests.

The first stop was Edwards Air Force Base in the Mojave Desert of California, in January. Hours of takeoffs and landings were performed, as were brake operation tests. Like the 720, the 720B was burdened with excessive loads of 5,000 pounds above the maximum gross takeoff weight. Landings were performed at 190,000 pounds, more than 15,000 pounds over normal weight.

In early February 1961, the third American Airlines 720B (N7539A, msn 18025) was involved in simulated airline operations around the United States and Canada. Some 103 functional and reliability flights were performed to experience the effects of various climates on the aircraft and its new engines. The week-long trip took the 720B from the high altitudes of Colorado Springs, to intense snow, cold and ice in Omaha, Kansas City, New York and Montreal. Miami offered the opposite extreme with 75-degree heat and humidity. The tests were completed on February 23, 1961, with certification following in early March.

Cowlings off, the exposed Pratt & Whitney fan JT3D-1s provide a look at their power. Titles on the forward fuselage proclaim the aircraft type. (The Boeing Company Archives)

As part of functional and reliability tests, the third 720B was sent around North America to simulate airline operations. On the ramp at Colorado Springs, American Astrojet N7539A (msn 18025) carries *Flagship Iowa* titles. The American Airlines tradition of naming its aircraft was not carried over to the "B" model 720, and the state name was removed before entering service. (The Boeing Company Archives)

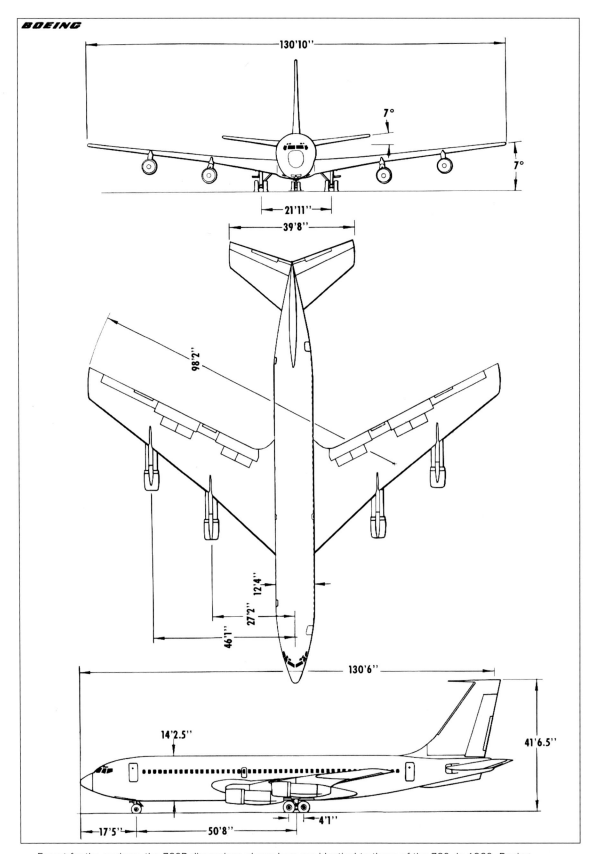

Except for the engines, the 720B dimensions shown here are identical to those of the 720. In 1960, Boeing completed studies for a proposed 720C model, for sale to British Overseas Airways Corporation (BOAC). It would have incorporated planned Rolls-Royce RB141.11A or Allison Rolls AR141-11B power plants. Exterior dimensions were to be identical to the earlier 720 models.

Nine years later, Boeing engineers studied the feasibility of converting surplus Eastern 720s to commercial short takeoff and landing (STOL) aircraft, referred to as the 720 C/STOL. Envisioned for operations from northeastern U.S. airports, the heavily modified airplane was to operate from 2,500-foot runways, carrying a maximum of 150 passengers on segments not exceeding 500 miles. To achieve such a lofty goal, four swing-out, suppressed-jet booster engines would augment four quiet-nacelle JT3D-7 power plants on takeoff. Like the first 720C proposal, the STOL design never made it beyond the drawing board. (The Boeing Company Archives)

A classic symbol of the Jet Age: the bold, impressive tail of the Boeing 720. Immaculately finished in red, white, blue and gold, the elegant livery of Eastern's first Boeing jet (msn 18155) epitomizes an era in commercial aviation long since past. (The Boeing Company Archives)

Boeing delivered a total of 154 new 720 and 720B aircraft to 17 different operators around the world. All but one of these customers were commercial airlines, with the Federal Aviation Agency taking possession of a single aircraft for training its flight safety inspectors. Because of its relatively low purchase price, the 720 provided airlines the ability to add jet-powered aircraft to their fleets. The 720s ordered by Aer Lingus, AVIANCA, Ethiopian, Pakistan International, Pacific Northern, Saudi Arabian and Western were the first turbine-jet aircraft purchased by these customers (although Western leased two 707s prior to receiving its own 720B aircraft). For Boeing, the continuing satisfaction of its 720 operators was just as important as making the sale. With the exception of Pacific Northern, which merged with Western in 1966, every one of the 720 customers went on to buy additional Boeing

jets. Perhaps more satisfying was the lock that Boeing held on the medium-range aircraft market; 75% of the original 720 owners purchased an additional 996 of the 727 tri-jets.

On average, a 720 would serve with its initial owner for just over 10 years before transfer to a secondary operator or being broken up for spares. Of the 154 aircraft delivered to the initial operators, seven aircraft were written off in accidents (which claimed 175 lives), 20 were sold for scrap and spares, and 127 went on to further service.

The following pages of this chapter illustrate how the first owners furnished and used the Boeing 720s and 720Bs, and provide a brief history of each customer. The section is organized in alphabetical order and not by any criteria such as the largest fleet or precedence of orders.

The first of three Boeing 720s for the Irish carrier is seen on rollout at Renton. The sharp, green-and-white livery suited the classic lines of the airliner. Aer Lingus placed only the "Boeing" inscription near the aft entry door, without the model designation. (The Boeing Company Archives)

Aer Lingus – Irish International Airlines

Formed by the Irish government, Aer Lingus Teoranta began service on May 27, 1936, with an inaugural flight from Dublin to Bristol, England. The name Aer Lingus was derived from the anglicization of "aerloingeas," which is Irish for "air fleet." The new airline briefly ceased operations at the start of World War II, resuming limited service from Ireland to England about a month later. After the end of hostilities, Aer Lingus expanded its European route network to include destinations in France and the Netherlands. In 1947, the country's first trans-Atlantic service was scheduled to begin, operated by a new associate carrier, Aerlinte Éireann (Irish Air Lines). After numerous problems with equipment and funding delays, the government indefinitely shelved plans for routes to North America. Its fleet of five new Lockheed 749 Constellations, much too large for economical use on flights to England and the continent, went to

BOAC the following year. Although its plans for Atlantic flights had ceased indefinitely, Aer Lingus continued to expand its routes throughout the European continent. Resurrected again, Aerlinte Éireann began service

A large crowd welcomes Archbishop Thomas A. Connolly after the blessing of *Pádraig* (St. Patrick) at Boeing Field in Seattle. (The Boeing Company Archives)

First-class passengers had a choice of 16 "instantly adjustable" seats in the forward cabin. Elegant meals were served on fine china set on embroidered Irish linen tablecloths.
(Museum of Flight Archives)

Across the Atlantic, economy-class passengers received Silver Shamrock service as they sat in a "living room in the sky."
(Museum of Flight Archives)

Plenty of libations, cigarettes and good company awaited first-class passengers in the forward Golden Shamrock Lounge.
(Museum of Flight Archives)

from Dublin via Shannon to New York in April 1958. Its trans-Atlantic fleet consisted of four leased 1049 Super Constellations from Seaboard and Western Airlines. Results after just 10 months of operation were encouraging; more than 13,000 passengers flew between Ireland and the United States, and the airline had expectations of tripling those numbers within two years. The Irish began service over the North Atlantic to the United States at the same time as the first Boeing jets were rolling off the assembly line. Aer Lingus management weighed the costs of obtaining an expensive fleet of jets against staying a bit longer with the older, piston-powered airliners. Its research indicated that with the anticipated increase in passenger traffic, the size, speed and economy of the jet airliners would more than justify the investment.

The news of a potential sale of the 720 to an international carrier came in early March 1959 through announcements on the wire services. These reports stated that the Irish government planned to recommend the purchase of three 720s for use on the Aer Lingus' New York–Shannon–Rome route. Boeing confirmed the order on March 13, 1959, stating that the airline called the 720 "the most suitable type" for its needs. As ordered, the jets had a maximum cruising speed of 615 miles per hour and a full passenger payload range of 3,550 miles, just enough for the nonstop, 3,000-mile trans-Atlantic flight from Shannon to New York. This range, along with lower sales and operating costs, made the new 720 a good choice for the growing airline.

The first "Shamrock Jet" rolled out of the paint hangar in its new emerald green and white on September 28, 1960. Earlier that year, to reflect its growth, Irish Air Lines became Irish International Airlines. The carrier's first 720, EI-ALA, was given the name *Pádraig* (St. Patrick) in honor of the patron saint of Ireland. The first flight took place on October 14, 1960, from the factory in Renton to Boeing Field in Seattle. Aircraft delivery ceremonies on October 26 included a blessing by Archbishop Thomas A. Connolly of the Catholic Diocese of Seattle. The 720 then flew south to Tucson, Arizona for crew orientation, where it was kept busy. During flight crew training,

14 Irish pilots took turns flying the 720 an average of 12 hours each day for 18 days. In one 24-hour period, these pilots set a record in daily jetliner utilization with 15 hours, 27 minutes.

Another record would fall during the ferry flight to Dublin. On November 19, aided by tailwinds that raised the 720's ground speed to 800 miles an hour, the 66 passengers aboard EI-ALA crossed the Atlantic from New York to Shannon in 4 hours, 58 minutes. A December westbound trial flight met these winds head-on, requiring a fueling stop in Gander, Newfoundland. Unfortunately, these intermediate fuel stops became a common occurrence on 720 flights to America, especially during the stormy winter months.

The second aircraft, named *Brigid* (also an Irish saint), made its first flight on December 20, 1960. Registered EI-ALB, it was delivered on January 24, 1961. The final Irish 720, EI-ALC, made its debut in a big way on April 7, 1961. Flown on the polar route from Seattle to Dublin, *Breandán* (St. Brendan) completed the 4,550-mile journey in 9 hours, 2 minutes. This delivery flight was the longest to date for the 720.

The airline had submitted its order anticipating that the first of the three deliveries would take place in late 1960 or early 1961, with an aircraft in service by early summer 1961. Scheduled flights for the 720 actually began on December 14, 1960, with the inaugural trip from Dublin to New York via Shannon. Aer Lingus initially offered three flights per week in each direction. The westbound service departed Dublin on Wednesdays and Saturdays (via Shannon and Boston to New York), as well as on Fridays (New York via Shannon only). The eastbound overnight return flights to Dublin were also made on Wednesday and Saturday (through Boston and Shannon) and Friday (via Shannon only). Within months, demand for the flights caused Aer Lingus to expand to daily trans-Atlantic service. The 720's speed and capacity became very useful on the route between Dublin and London, starting in the summer of 1961. During that year, the airline also operated a number of 720 flights for El Al on the London-Tel Aviv route. At that time, roundtrip fares from New York to Dublin were listed as $864.80 for

Aer Lingus		
Registration	msn	Name
EI-ALA	18041	*Pádraig*
EI-ALB	18042	*Brigid*
EI-ALC	18043	*Breandán*

EI-ALA between flights at New York's JFK Airport in September 1966. Although the basic colors remained unchanged from delivery, the large Aer Lingus titles reflected the airline's Irish identity. (Harry Sievers)

EI-ALA, now named *St. Pappin,* returns to Aer Lingus service after being repossessed from Trans Polar. The Irish airline restored the fuselage titles, leaving the tail white and the cheatline in Trans Polar blue. The aircraft taxies at Paris-Le Bourget in 1972. (Harry Sievers)

first-class and $458 in economy. A 17-day, economy-class excursion fare was also available for $322. Boston fares were slightly less expensive at $848.60, $449 and $315 respectively.

The Aer Lingus 720s provided two classes of service. The 16 passengers in the forward, first-class cabin enjoyed "Golden Shamrock service" that included gourmet meals set with embroidered Irish linens, Waterford crystal and Royal Tara china. After dinner, the hospitality continued with a selection of liqueurs served up front in the Golden Shamrock lounge. In keeping with the theme, economy-class passengers were offered "Silver Shamrock service." Six-abreast seating was available for 101 passengers who could "relax across the Atlantic enjoying man-sized meals, excellent bar service, and the gracious attention of six friendly Irish hostesses."

Designed by the American consulting firm of Walter Dorwin Teague, the cabin decor featured seats in alternating rows of green and gold. The cabin panels were "representative of an Irish stone wall" with the customary shamrocks scattered throughout. The partition between first class and economy was made of six square yards of Carrickmacross lace laminated in plastic panels. The bulkhead separating the forward cabin from the lounge featured a stylized mural of the map of Ireland. The original cabin layout provided two forward and two aft lavatories for the 117 passengers.

Despite range limitations, the three Aer Lingus 720s performed well as trans-Atlantic airliners. Although flying over the ocean was better suited for longer-range aircraft, the 720 provided Ireland with an early and economical entry into an exclusive club of jet operators. In 1963, following a fire on the ocean liner *Canberra,* the airline's chartered 720s ferried passengers back to Melbourne, Australia. Two 720s were pressed into service for this contract. EI-ALC was also leased to Pakistan International Airways from October 19, 1963 until the following May to operate its London-Karachi route.

To meet growing demand, Aer Lingus received the first of its fleet of four intercontinental 707-348Cs in June 1964. An additional 707 arrived from Boeing each year for the next three years, making the 720 fleet somewhat expendable.

The first to leave was EI-ALB, leased to Braniff International on September 15, 1964, with an option to buy. EI-ALC was the next to depart,

leased on a short-term basis to several airlines, including Pakistan International, Braniff, British West Indian and Trans Caribbean. It was finally sold to Trans Polar on November 1, 1970. Renamed *Hjalmer Riis-Larsen,* it would be repossessed and returned to service with Aer Lingus six months later. Trans European purchased and reregistered the aircraft in August 1972.

EI-ALA served Aer Lingus for five years before being leased to Braniff and El Al. Like its sister, it was sold to Trans Polar in 1970, renamed *Roald Amundsen* (LN-TUU). Repossessed, it returned to the Irish airline on May 18, 1971, and christened *St. Pappin.* American Aviation Services bought the 720 in October 1972.

Aer Lingus had a great deal of faith that the 720 could perform well over its North Atlantic routes and draw substantial numbers of passengers on flights to and from Ireland. Purchased as a less expensive alternative to the 707, the airline grew quickly with its 720s and, within a few years, found itself needing larger aircraft to meet traffic demands. The Boeing 720 remains a significant aircraft in the history of Irish aviation, responsible for bringing the Jet Age to the Emerald Isle.

In summer 1961, the Irish government issued the first postage stamps to feature the Boeing 720. Two stamps, printed in both blue and green, commemorated the 25th anniversary of the founding of Aer Lingus. The carrier's first aircraft, a de Havilland Dragon DH-84 (EI-ABI) was pictured along with the Dublin airport terminal building. The 720 appears on the upper right corner with registration EI-ALA clearly visible on tail. (Brian Baum Collection)

Missing its vertical fin, American's first 720-023 is towed on the ramp at Renton. (The Boeing Company Archives)

American Airlines

American Airlines (AA) was a staunch Douglas customer from early on. The airline's president, C.R. Smith, convinced Donald Douglas to build the DC-3 even when the manufacturer was enjoying robust sales of its smaller DC-2. Surplus military (C-54) versions of the DC-4 followed, and later American built a large fleet of DC-6 and DC-7 transports. Although twin-engine Convair 240s would replace DC-3s on American's short-haul services, it was assumed by most that the airline's managers would select the DC-8 for its first jet services. Boeing's only success with American consisted of a small order for double-deck 377 Stratocruisers to be used on its American Overseas Airlines subsidiary's trans-Atlantic routes.

Instead, American chose Boeing, placing a $135-million order for 30 of the domestic 707-100 variants in November 1955. Then, on July 30, 1958, long before the first American 707 arrived, C.R. Smith announced an order for 25 Boeing 720s, plus an option for 25 more. At the same time, the 707 order was reduced from 30 to 25. This initial press release stated that the airline would refer to its 720 as the "707-023." Also ordered at this time were 25 Convair 600 jetliners, later to be renamed the 990. With 35 Lockheed 188 Electras on the books as well, American was committed to a total of $365 million in new aircraft orders.

Although the first 707 deliveries began in late 1958, a pilot strike delayed service startup until January 25, 1959, when American became the third airline to operate the type (behind Pan American and National, which leased 707s from Pan Am). American was the first U.S. carrier to fly jets across the country, between Los Angeles and New York. All 25 707-123s were delivered by November 1959.

American's 707s, deployed on major transcontinental nonstop and Chicago–West Coast routes, replaced relatively young Douglas DC-7 and DC-7B variants. Electra service

preceded the 707 by two days, and began superseding DC-6 and DC-6B aircraft in addition to the DC-7. Some of the DC-7Bs were immediately relegated to cargo conversions, while another 25 DC-7s were sold and left American first during the first five months of 1959.

To upgrade its Boeing jet fleet, American reached an agreement with the manufacturer in July 1959 to upgrade its 707s and 720s to "B" models with new Pratt & Whitney turbofan engines. Twenty-three 707s were so converted (two were lost in training accidents prior to conversion) and a 26th, to replace one of the lost aircraft, was delivered with turbofan power. Savings resulting from lower fuel consumption were a major benefit of the turbofan power plants, but the added power became every bit as important to the decision makers who approved the program.

In order to maintain delivery schedules, the first 10 720-023s were produced with conventional JT3C-7 turbojet engines and later retrofitted

Wearing its *Flagship Connecticut* name, N7528A was delivered to American on June 24, 1960. Notice the small, forward lavatory porthole windows, an AA trademark on its first-generation Boeing jets. (The Boeing Company Archives)

with modified JT3D-1-MC7 turbofans. The last 15 720s came equipped with new JT3D-1 turbofan power plants. The upgraded JT3D-1-MC6 and -MC7 engines that powered the 707s and 720s, along with the new JT3D-1 model, were brought to a common 17,000-pound thrust rating (at 59 degrees Fahrenheit), producing fleet commonality with engines that were interchangeable.

While American undertook the engine conversion program in house, Boeing modified the airframes. In conjunction with the engine upgrade, the 707s received extensions to the vertical fin and horizontal stabilizers.

A leading-edge extension to the wing was installed between the inboard engine strut and the body, plus full-span leading-edge flaps. The addition of a ventral fin on the underside of the aft body completed the major changes. The 720 had most of these improvements incorporated into its original construction and only needed horizontal tail mods and the new engines.

N7538A was the first 720B delivered to American, on February 2, 1961, thus receiving much of the publicity exposure. This staged photo reflects the new "Astrojet" markings on the aft fuselage and tail. (The Boeing Company Archives)

The early Jet Age saw quantum leaps in passenger traffic, so American was happy to receive the first of its new 720-023s on July 24, 1960. A week later, on July 31, the type opened "Jet Gateway" service between Cleveland and Los Angeles via St. Louis. Rapid 720 deliveries allowed expansion of jet flights to additional cities on the AA route system. New York-Idlewild–Chicago service was added on August 14, followed by a New York–San Diego route via Chicago and Phoenix on August 27. New York–Chicago service was quickly increased to five daily roundtrips.

American's N7536A was the last of 10 720-023s delivered. It appears following conversion to turbofan power, dressed in the airline's circle-logo livery, introduced in 1963. (Mel Lawrence photo/Bryant Petitt Jr. Collection)

American's 720s were marketed as "707-720s" and carried 707 Jet Flagship titles. The type initially seated 98 passengers with 48 first-class and 50 coach seats. A forward, six-seat lounge was provided for first-class customers, but per a long-standing rule at the airline, these seats were not offered for sale.

First-class capacity would gradually be reduced as coach travel became more popular. By 1963, 32 first-class and 74 coach seats became the norm. Shortly thereafter, the forward lounge was removed in favor of six standard first-class seats.

When American updated its image in 1968, 720B N7528A was given the honor of being first to wear the new color scheme. This picture was taken at New York-JFK before the stylized eagle was applied to the tail. (Harry Sievers)

The first 720B, ordered by American Airlines, made a 2-hour, 56-minute shakedown-and-evaluation flight on October 6, 1960. Certification was obtained on March 3, 1961, and American placed the first of 15 720-023B models into commercial service on March 12. Initially the type operated from New York-Idlewild to Chicago-O'Hare and on to Mexico City. American also began phasing in its modified 707-123Bs on the same day, with a daily roundtrip on the highly competitive Los Angeles–New York route. Fan-powered aircraft were marketed as "Astrojets," ending a long tradition of individual Flagship names assigned to each airplane.

The 25th and final 720B delivery on July 25, 1961, completed American's initial 707/720 order. Of the first 215 Boeing jets delivered, American received 51. The airline was then operating the largest Boeing jet fleet in the world, and management had already signed a letter of intent for 25 tri-jet 727s with deliveries to begin in 1964.

Meanwhile, upgrading the non-fan Boeings was well under way. The first 707-123 entered the program on November 11, 1960, and the last was returned to service on February 1, 1962. The 720s began conversion in June 1961 with all 10 back on the line by November 14 of that year. Once the program was completed, the two types were more commonly scheduled and all public references were standardized behind the 707 Astrojet identity, both in print ads and timetables. By October 1961, fleet strength allowed introduction of Astrojet service on shorter routes such as Boston–Chicago, New York–Toronto, New York–Cincinnati, Phoenix–Los Angeles and Chicago–Dallas. The 720Bs also put in some work on transcontinental nonstop routes.

More 707-123Bs were acquired, along with intercontinental-range 707-323Bs and -323Cs; however, none of the optioned 720Bs were purchased, leaving the fleet at 25.

While American was well-satisfied with its 720s, the Convair 990s were a problem from the beginning. Deliveries were delayed until early 1962, well after the entire 720 fleet was in service, but high operating costs and lack of speed performance resulted in the variant's early withdrawal. The 990s were completely out of service by October 1968 and gradually sold off. Meanwhile, except for two aircraft, American's 720-023Bs did not begin leaving until late 1970 when three were sold to Middle East Airlines (MEA). In fact, MEA would eventually acquire a total of 13 ex-American 720Bs, some in exchange for the 990s originally purchased from

American. AA, in turn, sold the Convairs off to other companies without putting any back into revenue service.

In addition to MEA, American's 720s initially migrated to Aerocondor, Alyemda, the Dubai government, the Los Angeles Dodgers baseball club, Monarch, Pan Am and Somali. The last airplane was sold on June 1, 1976, closing more than 15 years of service without a fatal accident.

American Airlines			
Registration	Fleet No.	msn	Flagship Name
N7527A	527	18013	Mississippi
N7528A	528	18014	Connecticut
N7529A	529	18015	Wisconsin
N7530A	530	18016	Alabama
N7531A	531	18017	North Dakota
N7532A	532	18018	South Carolina
N7533A	533	18019	South Dakota
N7534A	534	18020	Colorado
N7535A	535	18021	Florida
N7536A	536	18022	Georgia
N7537A	537	18023	
N7538A	538	18024	
N7539A	539	18025	
N7540A	540	18026	
N7541A	541	18027	
N7542A	542	18028	
N7543A	543	18029	
N7544A	544	18030	
N7545A	545	18031	
N7546A	546	18032	
N7547A	547	18033	
N7548A	548	18034	
N7549A	549	18035	
N7550A	550	18036	
N7551A	551	18037	

N7527A–N7536A delivered as 720-023s; balance delivered as 720-023Bs

Flagship names were removed upon conversion to turbofan power.

N7548A approaches Los Angeles International in December 1969 with a non-standard Astrojet marking just behind the unpainted nose cone. (Harry Sievers)

A classic study of HK-724, taken in the Pacific Northwest. It was delivered to AVIANCA on November 8, 1961, and christened *Bolivar*. (The Boeing Company Archives)

AVIANCA
Aerovias Nacionales de Colombia

With a history traceable back to 1919, AVIANCA – Aerovias Nacionales de Colombia, is recognized as the oldest airline in the Americas and the second oldest after KLM. Having operated 10 Boeing 247Ds acquired from United in 1937, its ties to the Seattle manufacturer run deep.

In the late 1950s, Juan Pablo Ortega, president of the prosperous and well-run airline, ordered a study to determine what jet aircraft type should be acquired to replace his piston fleet that was flying a 32,000-mile system of domestic and international routes. AVIANCA linked Colombia with Miami and New York in the United States; Frankfurt, Lisbon, Madrid and Paris in Europe; and Caracas, Lima, Panama and Quito in South America. While most of the smaller cities could not support turbine service, there was a need for jets to replace Lockheed Constellations on the longer international routes.

On June 30, 1960, the airline announced an order for two 720-059B jetliners to be delivered in fall 1961. The total cost of the sale was $13.5 million, including spare engines and equipment. High-temperature, high-altitude airports on the AVIANCA route system, such as Quito, Ecuador (9,220 feet) and Bogota, Colombia (8,260 feet) prompted selection of turbofan-powered Boeings.

Anxious to establish jet service in advance of the delivery of the 720s, AVIANCA reached an agreement with Pan American to lease a 707 for service between Bogota and New York beginning on October 16, 1960. At that time, the important international route involved more than 11 hours and three intermediate stops aboard the carrier's Lockheed Super Constellations. Jet service, with a planned single stop in Jamaica, would cut that time almost in half.

AVIANCA's 720Bs were named after legendary names in Colombian history. HK-724 was christened *Bolivar*, after Simon Bolivar, the liberator of South America. *Santander*, HK-725, was named after General Francisco de Paula Santander, vice-president of Gran Colombia – the short-lived union of Colombia, Ecuador and Venezuela. AVIANCA configured the first-class cabin with 32 seats and a six-place lounge. Tourist-class seated 75.

The airline's first 720B was delivered on November 8, 1961, and began revenue flying November 24 on a weekly service between New York and

		AVIANCA	
Registration	**msn**	**Model**	**Name**
HK-676*	18059	030B	*Francisco Antonia Rea*
HK-677*	18057	030B	*Liborio Mejia*
HK-723**	18061	047B	*Ricaurte*
HK-724	18086	059B	*Bolivar*
HK-725	18087	059B	*Santander*
HK-726	18831	059B	*Narino*
HK-749*	18248	030B	*Antonio Baraya*

* Purchased from Lufthansa
** Purchased from Western

HK-724 displays modified AVIANCA colors in this June 1970 photo taken at New York-JFK. (Harry Sievers)

Bogota, stopping at Miami as well as Montego Bay and Kingston. Increased frequencies followed with the delivery of the second aircraft on November 16. By January 1962, five weekly flights included a New York–Bogota nonstop plus two services via Miami and Kingston, and two New York–Montego Bay–Kingston–Bogota routings. All of the flights continued from Bogota to Quito and/or Lima. Bogota–Caracas flights operated twice weekly.

This classic setting at the New York-JFK International Arrivals Building in December 1965 includes AVIANCA's HK-725 *Santander,* still in its original colors four years after delivery. (Harry Sievers)

The jet's speed advantage was not a major factor in ticket pricing, however. In 1962, a roundtrip first-class ticket from Miami to Bogota aboard one of the remaining Super Constellation flights cost $296, compared to $316 for 720B service.

AVIANCA also commenced a pooling agreement with Air France in early 1962, operating a weekly 720B flight from Bogota to Frankfurt via Caracas, San Juan, Madrid and Paris, while Air France flew a slightly different routing twice weekly with Boeing 707-328s. On an early AVIANCA service, the San Juan–Madrid segment, 4,050 miles, was flown in a record time of 6 hours and 32 minutes.

A third 720B was ordered in May 1964 for additional service on existing jet routes. HK-726 was christened *Narino,* after Don Antonio Narino, considered the most important forefather of Colombian independence. It was delivered on April 6, 1965, and joined the fleet two days later.

For domestic routes, AVIANCA chose the Boeing 727, which entered service on January 1, 1966. As it continued to grow, the carrier took delivery of a long-range 707-359B in 1968, mainly for use on its trans-Atlantic service, and another in 1970; five more ex-Pan Am 707s would later be acquired. A 720-047B was purchased from Western Airlines following the addition of a new route to Los Angeles in July 1969.

Shedding a color scheme that dated back to the carrier's majority ownership by Pan Am soon after World War II, AVIANCA introduced a bright new red livery in 1970.

The company continued its growth, including added European destinations. From the used market, three 720-030Bs were acquired, one at the end of 1972 and two more in 1973. Originally delivered to Lufthansa, the trio flew for Pan Am before joining AVIANCA.

More modern and spacious jets gradually replaced the 720B fleet. In addition, HK-723 was damaged beyond economical repair during a landing accident at Mexico City in 1976, and HK-725 met a similar fate when it ran off the runway while landing at Quito in 1980. The three 720-030Bs were leased to AVIANCA's partner carrier, Sociedad Aeronautica de Medellin, S.A. (SAM) in 1977, and did not return prior to being retired. The last two airplanes were finally withdrawn from AVIANCA service in July 1983.

AVIANCA unveiled a striking new look in 1970. HK-726 *Narino* shows off the bright red livery at New York-JFK. (Harry Sievers)

Retired from service and stored in 1981, HK-749 sat neglected for more than six years. The aircraft was then disassembled and moved to the Museo de Los Niños, a children's museum at Bogota. It was restored without engines, in AVIANCA's latest colors. (via Nicky Scherrer)

Thought to be one of the most attractive liveries ever, Braniff's first jet colors are a perfect fit on N7076. (The Boeing Company Archives)

Braniff International Airways

Another longtime Douglas customer, Braniff International Airways was one of the few major carriers to retain the name of its founder, Paul R. Braniff. From a combination airplane distributor, aircraft parts dealer, flying school and airline formed in 1928, the company evolved as a major U.S. airline. By 1956, its routes stretched through America's Midwest heartland and included service from Texas to northeast destinations plus flights to Central and South America.

In 1955, Braniff managers chose Lockheed's turboprop model 188 Electra to replace Convair twins and Douglas DC-6 equipment on short- to medium-range flights. Nine Electras were ordered; another would be acquired later, plus one on lease.

For major routes in the United States and Latin America, the airline shopped around but settled on a unique variant of the Boeing 707. In desire of the 707-100's capacity and increased power, Boeing produced the 707-200, which utilized the -100 fuselage length plus the larger Pratt & Whitney JT4A-3 turbojet engine normally fitted to the intercontinental 707-320 airframe. The resulting 707-227 "El Dorado Super Jet" met the company's requirements for improved takeoff performance needed at some of Braniff's high-altitude airports and increased cruising speed desired for marketing purposes. An order for five was announced on December 1, 1955.

The first aircraft in the order, N7071, crashed during an acceptance flight in October 1959, resulting in the deaths of four aboard, while four others survived. The second aircraft was delivered to Braniff on December 3 and entered service two weeks later between Dallas and New York. A Dallas–Chicago roundtrip commenced on the same day. Braniff experienced only two mechanical delays during its first 60 days of 707 operations.

San Antonio was added to the 707 schedule in March 1960, followed by Central and South America flights from the East Coast a month later when the fourth 707 entered revenue service. Piston equipment was "stair-stepped," with DC-7Cs replacing DC-6s, allowing that type to replace

Convair 340s and 440s, which permitted the last of Braniff's DC-3s to be retired by mid-May.

With the 707s performing flawlessly, Braniff President Charles Beard looked to purchase more jetliners for medium-length routes. After seriously considering the Convair 880, Braniff ordered three Boeing 720-027s on March 8, 1960, to supplement the four 707-227s (the 707 accident aircraft was not replaced). Deliveries would commence in February 1961. While the Convair jets offered speed and competitive seat-mile costs, the 720's commonality won the order for Boeing.

To remain flexible with the larger 707s during initial service, it was planned that the two models would have identical 50 first-class and 56 coach layouts, but the 720s would lack the first-class lounge. Delivery of the third aircraft was later put back, meaning that only two would be in operation for several months.

Braniff's first 720 entered service on February 20, 1961, on routes previously flown by the 707s. Its recognized inaugural was from Chicago-O'Hare to Dallas and San Antonio. The second airplane arrived on March 22, and on April 30, replaced an Electra on the Minneapolis/ St. Paul–Kansas City–Dallas–San Antonio–Mexico City route. Boeing 720 flights between Houston and Denver via Dallas commenced in June. An option for a fourth aircraft was taken up less than two months after the type entered service, followed a year later by a fifth firm order. The last two 720-027s would join the fleet in May 1962 and August 1963, respectively. They replaced some 707-227 domestic services as those aircraft were reassigned to South American routes. By fall 1963, the last DC-7C was withdrawn from Latin American service, and all Braniff flights between North and South America were flown with jets.

For additional capacity, a 720-048 was purchased from Aer Lingus in 1964. By this time, Braniff was looking to become an all-jet airline. It would be the first U.S. carrier to order British-built BAC 1-11 jets, placing the type into short-haul domestic service in April 1965. Boeing 727-27C "quick-change" tri-jets were ordered in 1965, and intercontinental 707-327Cs began arriving in mid-1966. Pan American-Grace Airways

Braniff's "End of the Plain Plane" promotion included solid-color liveries. In addition to the colors shown, the 720s appeared in periwinkle blue, medium blue, ochre and yellow.

N7076 - dark blue (Harry Sievers)

N7079 - orange (Harry Sievers)

N7080 - beige (Manuel Delgado)

Later two-tone color schemes included this red and pumpkin livery, seen in May 1973 on N7077, shortly before it left Braniff's fleet. Visible are crown skin reinforcement stringers on top of the fuselage. (Harry Sievers Collection)

(PANAGRA) was acquired in January 1967, bringing early model DC-8s into the fleet. Four used 707-138Bs were added in 1969. With Braniff's route map stretching in all directions, DC-8-62s were added in the late 1960s, and 727-227s began arriving in 1970 followed by its first Boeing 747 that same year. Braniff was flying a wide variety of fleet types.

Meanwhile, the 720s soldiered on. Two more Aer Lingus 720-048s had been leased from November 1965 until May 1966. A month later, the 720-048 purchased earlier was sold to Pacific Northern Airlines. A final 720 saw service with the airline for eight months in 1972. N7224U, a 720-022, was leased from United, again for extra fleet capacity.

In 1973, the remaining five 720s, all factory deliveries, were sold in one batch to American Aviation Services, Inc. for use by Aeroamerica. All were out of the fleet by October 30. As it turned out, the 720s outlasted the 707-227s at Braniff by two years.

| | | | Braniff | |
Registration	Fleet No.	msn	Model	Notes
N7076	076	18064	027	
N7077	077	18065	027	
N7078	078	18154	027	
N7079	079	18423	027	
N7080	080	18581	027	
N7081	081	18042	048	Purchased from Aer Lingus
N7082	082	18043	048	Leased 11/1/65 to 5/24/66
N7083	083	18041	048	Leased 11/15/65 to 5/15/66
N7224U	- -	18077	022	Leased 5/6/72 to 12/31/72

Delivered on March 22, 1961, N7077 was the second 720 to join Braniff's fleet. (The Boeing Company Archives)

Rollout of Continental's first 720B also debuted a modification to the airline's "Golden Jet" livery with this black-and-gold scheme that would spread to the 707 fleet. (The Boeing Company Archives)

Continental Airlines

Continental Airlines traces its history back to Varney Air Transport, which, in 1934, began flying four-stop service between Denver and El Paso with a Lockheed Vega. Renamed Continental Air Lines three years later, the carrier was under the control of legendary Robert F. Six, whose reign would last 46 years.

In November 1955, the U.S. Civil Aeronautics Board (CAB) shocked the industry with major new route awards when deciding its Denver Service Case. The board granted Continental a route from Los Angeles to Chicago via Denver and Kansas City, including nonstop authority between all city pairs. This elevated the airline from a short-haul carrier to a major player in the airline industry.

Six immediately ordered four Boeing 707-124s (later increased to five) for delivery in 1959, along with 15 Vickers Viscount 800s. Facing a three-year wait for the Viscounts and nearly four years for the 707s, he also ordered five Douglas DC-7Bs for interim service on the new routes. Until then, Continental's fleet consisted of DC-6B, Convair twin and DC-3 equipment. Its longest routes were interchange segments flown with several carriers.

The first 707-124 "Golden Jet" debuted on June 8, 1959, flying Continental's flagship Los Angeles–Chicago nonstop route. Three daily 707 roundtrips were operating within two weeks of the inaugural flight. Denver and Kansas City flights began in August, and six daily California–Chicago roundtrips were flying by September 5.

The CAB triggered another aircraft order in March 1961 when it awarded to Continental the coveted Los Angeles–Houston route, via Phoenix, Tucson, El Paso and San Antonio as part of the Southern Transcontinental Route Case. Again, nonstop authority was granted between all points. Formerly flown as an interchange service with American Airlines, this new award quickly increased Continental's route mileage. Service began on June 11; Continental's fifth 707,

recently delivered, operated some of the flights. Four days later, Continental announced that it would buy four Boeing 720-024Bs to beef up its new California–Texas service.

The slightly smaller Boeings were chosen as the right fit for the mission, both in terms of capacity and improved takeoff performance at several hot-weather destinations. While waiting for the 720Bs, the airline's 707s were utilized at an average rate of 10.8 hours daily. With this kind of work schedule, one of the aircraft became the first jetliner to fly 10,000 hours. N70773 reached the milestone in November 1961.

The first 720B was delivered on April 30, 1962, followed by a second on May 27. Just as the capacity was added to the fleet, a 707-124 crashed on May 22, the victim of sabotage. The two 720B Golden Jets quickly entered service on routes from California to both Chicago and Texas, followed by a third aircraft delivered on June 20. In July, a fifth 720B was ordered to replace the lost 707. Another single-aircraft order followed three months later.

Continental's 720Bs were configured with 40 first-class and 74 "Club Coach" seats, while the 707s by then seated 40 in the front and 88 aft. First-class capacity in both aircraft included six forward lounge seats, while the 707s featured a four-seat coach lounge as well. By mid-summer 1962,

A large crowd turned out to see this Continental 720B bring the first pure-jet service to Midland/Odessa, Texas in 1962. (The Boeing Company Archives)

Continental's "meatball" colors appeared on the 720B fleet, as evidenced by this shot of N17207 on approach to Los Angeles in October 1971. (Harry Sievers)

Golden Jet 707 and 720B routes included the original California–Chicago segments, Los Angeles nonstops to San Antonio and Houston, Dallas–Midland/Odessa–Albuquerque–Denver and Dallas–El Paso. As additional 720Bs arrived, service was added to other cities, including Phoenix, Tucson and Amarillo. The remaining DC-7Bs and DC-6Bs were phased out while a single DC-3 continued to shuttle passengers between Denver and Colorado Springs until September 1965.

In July 1964, Continental ordered two convertible, passenger-cargo 707-324C jets for military contract work related to the Vietnam War. However, the airline's management still felt the need for smaller-capacity jets and, on March 1, 1965, ordered two additional 720Bs, to bring that fleet to eight aircraft. For short segments,

Continental		
Registration	Fleet No.	msn
N57201	201	18416
N57202	202	18417
N57203	203	18418
N57204	204	18419
N57205	205	18587
N57206	206	18763
N17207	207	19002
N17208	208	19003

DC-9-10C equipment replaced the Viscounts beginning in April 1966.

A second 707-124 was lost at Kansas City in 1965, and the remaining three were sold to TWA in 1967. But the 720B fleet continued to serve Continental well into the 1970s, even as the airline maintained its rapid expansion and acquired widebody jets. The first 720B to leave was N57203, sold to Ethiopian Airlines in September 1973. Another two would go to the same carrier in 1974, but the remaining aircraft were kept busy, with one 720B performing the first East Coast service to Miami on June 1, 1974.

Finally, the last five 720-024Bs were retired in the spring of 1976. Sold to Allen Aircraft Corporation, they were broken up.

N57203 strikes a classic pose over Puget Sound near Seattle, during a pre-delivery flight. (The Boeing Company Archives)

Eastern's first 720 sits on the ramp at Renton, shortly after leaving the paint hangar; its cockpit windows are still masked over. Titles near each of the two main cabin doors announced that first-class passengers would experience "Golden Falcon Service," while those entering via the aft entrance enjoyed "Deluxe Coach Service." (Museum of Flight/Gordon Williams Collection)

Eastern Air Lines

Pioneering U.S. carrier Eastern Air Lines operated every variety of postwar propliner built by Douglas except one. It flew the DC-2, DC-3, DC-4, DC-6B and DC-7B. Several varieties of the Lockheed Constellation were acquired, plus Convair 440s and the Martin 404. Claiming no exclusive aircraft manufacturer relationship, Eastern Chairman and World War I ace Eddie Rickenbacker visited all the major builders in search of turbine equipment best suited for Eastern's route system that existed almost exclusively east of the Mississippi River and included points in Canada, Mexico, Bermuda and the Caribbean.

With a myriad of short-haul routes, it was not surprising that Rickenbacker selected the Lockheed 188 Electra for the first phase of fleet modernization. A launch customer for the type, Eastern bought 40 on February 9, 1956; options for an additional 30 were not taken up, although one additional Electra was eventually acquired. The first production model was delivered to Eastern in October 1958, but service did not begin until early 1959.

The DC-8 was chosen for Eastern's longer sectors, with an order signed in December 1955 for 18 airplanes, plus eight options. Deliveries were to begin in May 1959 with the first six aircraft to be domestic Series 10 versions, followed by 12 DC-8-21s with more powerful JT4 engines. When this power plant became available earlier than expected, Eastern's order was amended with all 18 to have the upgraded power. But two cancellations and release of one delivery position to Aeronaves de Mexico reduced the final number delivered to 15; the last was delivered in October 1961.

Production delays would push service startup back to January 24, 1960, on the New York-Idlewild–Miami run; Chicago–Miami service began in February. During 1960, DC-8 routes were predominantly from New York to Miami, New Orleans, San Juan, Atlanta, Houston, Bermuda, Tampa, West Palm Beach and Mexico City. Chicago–Atlanta–Miami, Boston–Miami, Boston–Philadelphia–Miami and Detroit–Miami rounded out the Douglas jet assignments.

On August 4, 1960, much to the delight of Boeing managers, Eastern finally broke the drought and announced an order for 10 720-025 jets to

Approaching its gate at New York-JFK in November 1964, N8711E still wears its original livery, but with shortened "Fly Eastern" fuselage titles. Behind the 720, a DC-8 in new colors awaits passengers. (Harry Sievers)

N8704E and a sister ship were both wearing the updated "hockey stick" scheme by the time this picture was taken in May 1965, again at JFK. (Mel Lawrence photo/Bryant Petitt Jr. Collection)

be delivered the following year. The $44-million investment was intended to complement the DC-8s and provide jet service on medium-haul routes. Eastern's 720s would be the only ones equipped with Pratt & Whitney JT3C-12 turbojets, each providing an additional 1,000 pounds of thrust over the standard JT3C-7s. The 720-025s were also ordered with two overwing exit doors instead of one on each side of the fuselage. This option allowed for high-density, 142-seat, all-coach configurations, although none of the aircraft were delivered with this seating plan.

Dramatic traffic growth prompted Eastern to increase its 720 order to 15 aircraft in October 1960, with the entire fleet expected in time for the 1961-62 winter season. Actually 13 were delivered to Eastern in 1961 plus an additional two a year later. The last to arrive, N8703E, was used as a flight-test vehicle by Boeing for several months and delivered out of sequence.

Regularly scheduled "Golden Falcon" 720 service commenced on September 24, 1961, on the New York-Idlewild–Jacksonville–Miami route, followed on October 1 by New York–Ft. Lauderdale flights, which the airline scheduled to operate in 2 hours, 23 minutes. New York–Jacksonville was another early 720 route. Rapid 720 deliveries produced an increased seat inventory while allowing retirement of piston aircraft to be accelerated. Lockheed Constellations were among the first to be withdrawn.

As Eastern began flying the 720, it already had a 40-plane order for Boeing's new 727 tri-jet with deliveries scheduled to begin in 1963. However, the four-engine Boeings would provide yeoman service not only for the next two years but well beyond the 727 debut. By 1967, the type was spread throughout Eastern's timetable, to 27 cities, with the heaviest schedules from New York and Newark, San Juan, Atlanta, Miami, New Orleans and Philadelphia. In addition to the routes mentioned above, it was flying such segments as Minneapolis/St. Paul–Chicago, Indianapolis–Louisville, Montreal–Newark, Bermuda–Washington-Dulles and Louisville–Newark.

Eastern chose new aircraft rather than upgrading its 720s to turbofan power plants. In 1969, managers were able to negotiate a gradual trade-in of the entire fleet to Boeing towards the purchase of 15 727-200 tri-jets. By

then, the airline had retired its last piston-powered variant, the Convair 440 (on July 1, 1969) and was flying 727-25s and convertible -25Cs as well as DC-9-10s and -30s.

Widebody jets were on order. Apparently unable to get a similar deal with Douglas, Eastern retained its DC-8-21 fleet until the early 1970s.

Boeing refurbished the 15 720s at its Wichita facility for resale to other customers. All were placed with a variety of airlines, travel clubs and charter operators including Aeroamerica, Calair, Conair, Korean Air Lines, Trans European, Trans Polar International and Voyager 1000.

Eastern		
Registration	Fleet No.	msn
N8701E	701	18155
N8702E	702	18156
N8703E	703	18157
N8704E	704	18158
N8705E	705	18159
N8706E	706	18160
N8707E	707	18161
N8708E	708	18162
N8709E	709	18163
N8710E	710	18164
N8711E	711	18240
N8712E	712	18241
N8713E	713	18242
N8714E	714	18243
N8715E	715	18244

The Eastern 720 fleet maintained a perfect safety record during its relatively short life. (The Boeing Company Archives)

Freshly painted in full El Al colors, 4X-ABA poses shortly before pre-delivery flight testing. It would later be sold and become one of the few 720 variants to receive a freighter conversion. (Museum of Flight/Gordon Williams Collection)

El Al Israel Airlines

The national airline of Israel, El Al, began operations in 1949 with two DC-4s converted from military C-54 standards. On July 31, 1949, weekly Tel Aviv–Paris roundtrip flights commenced, with a fuel stop in Rome. A year later, the fledgling airline began trans-Atlantic charter flights to New York with DC-4s making en route stops at Rome, Paris, Shannon and Gander. European service was also increased that year, and the first flight to Johannesburg, South Africa took place in November. For shorter segments, El Al relied on converted C-46 Commandos operating in both cargo and passenger configurations.

Early Model 49 Lockheed Constellations began replacing the DC-4s on long-haul services by the end of 1950 and inaugurated El Al's first regularly scheduled flights to New York on April 29, 1951. Eastbound Shannon stops were eliminated with the longer-range Connies, which now offered twice weekly Tel Aviv–New York roundtrips.

Four years later, the airline was still struggling along with its vintage Constellations. A decision was made to acquire three Bristol Britannia turboprop airliners for service to the United States. Although this type nearly doubled the seating capacity of a Connie and had nonstop trans-Atlantic range, it suffered from production delays and did not make an appearance at Tel Aviv until September 1957, several months late. But El Al had a winner on its hands. During one of the airline's proving flights, a Britannia completed the 5,760-mile New York–Tel Aviv sector nonstop in 14 hours, 46 minutes, a new record for the longest distance ever covered nonstop by a commercial land plane.

Regular Tel Aviv–London–New York service commenced on December 22, 1957, only three days after BOAC began its own London–New York Britannia flights. El Al's clever advertising exclaimed, "No Goose, no Gander," referring to the lack of refueling stops at Goose Bay, Labrador and Gander, Newfoundland, a virtual certainty on competitive airliners operating with conventional aircraft.

Now an established leader on the trans-Atlantic circuit, El Al's managers selected the Rolls-Royce-powered 707-458 to replace the Britannias. Two were ordered on March 1, 1960 with service planned to

A fine study of 4X-ABA, taken while the aircraft rested between flights at London's Heathrow Airport in 1971. (Terry Waddington Collection)

Aer Lingus applied El Al titles to EI-ALA while leasing it to the Israeli carrier. It was photographed at London-Heathrow in November 1968. (Harry Sievers)

begin during the summer of 1961. With competitive carriers putting pure jets against the El Al turboprops, it was decided to lease a VARIG 707-441 in order to commence a weekly one-stop Tel Aviv–New York roundtrip in January 1961. A second weekly flight was added in the following month. The eastbound inaugural flight was able to operate nonstop and set a new speed record in the process.

El Al's own 707s took over the route on June 10, 1961. With two new Boeing jets in its fleet, the carrier operated three weekly flights, one returning nonstop; all the remaining flights called on London or Paris en route. A third 707-458, ordered in February 1961, arrived in early 1962.

Even before El Al's 707s entered service, the airline recognized a need for additional jets to replace the last European Britannia service that had earlier permitted retirement of the last two El Al Constellations. Accordingly, a pair of Boeing 720-058Bs was ordered on May 4, 1961, for delivery a year later.

In addition to the task of fleet modernization, the 720B was chosen for its ability to complete another mission. Ever since the 1956 Sinai War, the Arab boycott forced El Al to utilize leased piston aircraft without company insignia in order to make its scheduled flights to Johannesburg, South Africa. This requirement made the route uneconomical and difficult to complete. But the 720B had sufficient range to fly between the cities via an exaggerated route with one stop at Tehran, Iran. The turbofan engines enabled takeoffs from the high elevations at both Tehran and Johannesburg, especially on hot days.

After flying east to Iran, the flights headed southwest across the Persian Gulf to Central Africa and on to Johannesburg. The circuitous routing added 2,400 miles to the trip and required an 85% load

factor to break even on costs for this 16-hour ordeal that included a minimum of 25 heading changes. Double crews staffed the 720Bs on these marathon trips.

The first 720-058B was delivered on March 26, 1962; the second came a month later. European routes were also flown with 720Bs, relegating the remaining two Britannias to supplementary service. In 1965, the 720B engines were upgraded from JT3D-1 to JT3D-3B standards for increased performance. Later that same year, El Al acquired a 707-358B. Two more -358Bs and two -358Cs would join the fleet by January 1970, when the first of the three 707-458s was retired.

As El Al grew, Boeing 737 twin-jets were purchased and leased for shorter segments, and 747-258Bs took over trans-Atlantic routes beginning in 1971. Leased Boeing 707s were utilized for short periods, along with two 720-048s, but the pair of 720Bs continued to provide reliable service over El Al's routes until both were withdrawn and sold in October 1980, closing out more than 18 years with their original owners.

El Al			
Registration	Fleet No.	msn	Model
4X-ABA	ABA	18424	058B
4X-ABB	ABB	18425	058B
EI-ALA*		18041	048
OO-TEB*		18043	048
*Leased from Aer Lingus			

Although El Al only bought two 720Bs, the aircraft provided valuable service for more than 18 years. (The Boeing Company Archives)

Ethiopian's distinctive livery has stood the test of time. First introduced on the DC-3s, the same basic design is still in use after more than 50 years. ET-AAG was named *White Nile*. (Museum of Flight/Gordon Williams Collection)

Ethiopian Airlines

Following World War II, the idea of a commercial aviation company in Ethiopia was discussed at the signing ceremony of the newly formed United Nations, held at San Francisco. When the American State Department was asked for help, a meeting was arranged between Ethiopia and officials of TWA, then still known as Transcontinental & Western Air. Just two months later, a contract between the two parties was completed, calling for TWA to purchase the aircraft and associated equipment while hiring flight crews, maintenance personnel and key managers to begin operations. With five military surplus C-47s, Ethiopian Air Lines (given the EAL moniker) operated its first regularly scheduled flight on April 8, 1946, from Addis Ababa to Cairo via Asmara.

Growing in a steady manner, Ethiopian added DC-3s and later Convair 240s while spreading its routes throughout Ethiopia and to surrounding countries in Africa and southern Europe. Although TWA's help was a major reason for the young airline's success, it was agreed that, ultimately, the entire operation would be taken over by Ethiopian personnel. As it grew, Ethiopian Air Lines took on a personality of its own, based on the country's warm hospitality and friendly service.

In a quantum leap, the carrier acquired three Douglas DC-6Bs in 1957, mainly for the purpose of inaugurating service to Frankfurt, an extension of its existing Addis Ababa–Cairo–Athens route. Three years later, EAL began a new service linking East and West Africa, between Addis Ababa and Monrovia, Liberia with intermediate stops at Khartoum and Accra. The airline also served Nairobi.

By 1960, EAL had completed 14 successful years without a passenger fatality and began examining options for the acquisition of jet airliners. The 720B was an obvious choice to serve Ethiopia's 7,500-foot-elevation airports at Addis Ababa and Asmara, although the Sud SE 210 Caravelle was also considered. The purchase of two 720-060Bs was announced on July 16, 1960, when a letter of intent was signed between Boeing and the

The Ethiopian 720B interiors were finished in warm colors. Sidewall coverings featured renderings of the Lalibela Church, the obelisks of Aksum and other landmarks of Ethiopia. Initially, the type was fitted with 32 first-class seats plus a six-seat lounge, and 71 in the economy section. (The Boeing Company Archives)

Traditional and native costumes make up the EAL flight attendant wardrobe, as seen during a delivery ceremony at Boeing Field, Seattle. (The Boeing Company Archives)

ET-ABP appears at Miami in February 1988, having been sold to AAR Allen Aircraft Corporation. It was re-registered as N440DS shortly after this picture was taken. The 720B would later become N7381 and eventually immigrate to the Ratheon Corporation. (Stefano Pagiola Collection)

	Ethopian		
Registration	**Fleet No.**	**msn**	**Model**
ET-AAG	AAG	18454	060B
ET-AAH	AAH	18455	060B
ET-ABP	ABP	18977	060B
ET-AFA*	AFA	18418	024B
ET-AFB*	AFB	18419	024B
ET-AFK*	AFK	18417	024B
*Purchased from Continental			

One of three 720Bs purchased secondhand, ET-AFB was still in basic Continental colors when photographed at New York-JFK in September 1974, en route to Ethiopia. TWA apparently performed some interior modifications to the aircraft. (Harry Sievers)

airline. Deliveries were planned for December 1961. However, by June of that year, delays in runway work at Asmara and the new airport at Addis Ababa forced the airline to put back acceptance of the new jets until October and November 1962. A new contract was drawn up, and the postponement opened two Boeing delivery positions that were taken up by Saudi Arabian Airlines.

Accepted by EAL in November 1962, the two 720Bs were flown together to Addis Ababa from Seattle via New York, Madrid and Athens, arriving within a few minutes of each other on December 3 at the brand-new Bole Airport. Inaugural jet service between Addis Ababa and Nairobi via Asmara commenced on January 15, 1963, with ET-AAH, named *Blue Nile*. On the following day, a new route to Madrid and Athens was initiated with the same aircraft that originated at Nairobi and flew up to Addis Ababa, again via Asmara.

Even as the new jets were entering service, Ethiopian beefed up its domestic fleet with six more DC-3s. The type would remain with the carrier until October 1991. In 1965, the company officially dropped its "Air Lines" spelling, adopting the more modern Ethiopian Airlines name. Continued route expansion, including new service in 1964 to Rome from Addis Ababa via Khartoum and Athens, justified acquisition of another 720-060B, which was delivered in September 1965.

A year later, two long-range 707-360C convertible passenger/cargo aircraft were ordered for deliveries beginning in 1968, the same year in which one of the 720Bs, ET-AAG, was destroyed by fire after a hard landing at Beirut while on lease to Middle East Airlines; there were no fatalities.

Even with the addition of 707 equipment, Ethiopian acquired three more 720Bs off the secondhand market. A 720-024B was purchased from Continental Airlines in October 1973, followed by two more in late 1974, bringing the 720B fleet total to five. Still considered a good fit to the EAL route map, the type remained through the 1970s. Ethiopian reportedly bought its first two medium-range 727-260s in 1979 to begin phasing the larger Boeings out. However, all of the 720Bs stayed on until November of 1985, a year after the airline's first two 767-260 (ER) variants had joined the fleet. ET-AFA and -AFB were sold to Boeing for use in the KC-135E upgrade program.

Another 720B was retired at the end of 1987, followed closely by the last two in 1988. Throughout 26 years with EAL, the 720Bs racked up an enviable record of service.

Ethiopian's factory-delivered 720Bs were equipped with an extra high-frequency (HF) antenna, protruding from the starboard wingtip leading edge, for increased radio capacity. (The Boeing Company Archives)

The FAA's lone 720, N113 (msn 18066) as seen at Renton before delivery. (The Boeing Company Archives)

Federal Aviation Agency

Making good on a letter of intent from the previous year, the U.S. Federal Aviation Agency (FAA) signed a firm contract to purchase a single Boeing 720 on January 26, 1961. Thanks to an order adjustment, the government only had to wait 106 days for the delivery of its new aircraft. Braniff International had signed up for three 720-027s on March 8, 1960, but it moved back the third aircraft delivery date, opening an earlier position on the production line. Originally planned to wear N7078 (Braniff would later use the registration on msn 18154), Boeing built it instead to Agency specifications.

N113 left the factory in FAA colors on April 10, 1961, and first flew on May 5, with delivery seven days later. The only 720 built that did not enter scheduled passenger service, it was utilized by the FAA for the training of safety inspectors. Federal policy dictated that its inspectors "have skill in aircraft equal to that of the airline pilots whose operations they monitor." Najeeb Halaby, FAA administrator, personally visited the Renton factory to check out the new jet, which remained in Seattle after delivery for 50 hours of pilot training.

Controlled Impact Demonstration

N113 would be sacrificed in spectacular fashion. See Chapter V. (NASA)

FAA Administrator Najeeb Halaby waves from the cockpit of N113. (The Boeing Company Archives)

Later christened *Koln,* D-ABOH awaits delivery to its owner. (The Boeing Company Archives)

Lufthansa German Airlines

Postwar Lufthansa German Airlines (LH) began operating in March 1955 with Convair 340s, soon followed by Lockheed Super Constellations. Trans-Atlantic service with 1049G Connies began in June as the airline stretched its wings in an effort to become a global carrier. Flights to South America, Africa and the Far East followed.

While Viscount turboprops continued a European expansion, Lockheed 1649A Starliners took over several long-haul LH services beginning in February 1958. Barely two years later, the first of four Rolls-Royce-powered intercontinental Boeing 707-430 jetliners was delivered. It was placed into service between Frankfurt and New York on March 17, 1960. The second 707 arrived in March, followed by the last two in April and October. Trans-Atlantic jet service was added on routes to Montreal, Chicago and San Francisco the same year; and in 1961, the 707s began flying from Frankfurt to Tokyo via Bangkok and Hong Kong.

In January 1960, Lufthansa became the first non-U.S. carrier to order 720Bs with a contract for four -030B variants; the order was increased to eight in November of the same year. The airplanes were purchased for service to the Middle East, the Orient and South America. Initially, it was planned to configure the interiors with 36 first-class and 66 tourist-class seats.

The first 720B was delivered to Lufthansa on March 8, 1961, and it entered service, following crew training, on May 20, flying a weekly South America service from Frankfurt to Santiago via Paris, Dakar, Rio de Janeiro, Sao Paulo and Buenos Aires. Five days later, a second weekly 720B service to Santiago began, with an added stop at Montevideo. On July 5, one flight began serving Zurich, dropping the Paris stop. The South American routes were operated as part of a pool agreement with Air France and Alitalia. The last Lufthansa Super G Constellation service on this sector ended shortly thereafter, along with Alitalia's final DC-6B flights, leaving two weekly roundtrips each with Lufthansa 720Bs, Air France 707s and Alitalia DC-8s.

The last of the original four 720Bs were received on June 3, 1961, allowing the July 1 inaugural of a route between Frankfurt and Tehran with two or three en route stops, depending on the day of the week. Intermediate cities included Munich, Vienna, Rome, Beirut, Cairo and Baghdad. The flight terminated and originated at Dhahran once a week. A daily Frankfurt–London 720B roundtrip was also added in November 1961.

Lufthansa		
Registration	msn	Name
D-ABOH	18057	Koln
D-ABOK	18058	Dusseldorf
D-ABOL	18059	Stuttgart
D-ABOM	18060	Nurnberg
D-ABON	18248	Hannover
D-ABOP	18249	Bremen
D-ABOQ	18250	Essen
D-ABOR	18251	Dortmund

Coming between January and March 1962, a second batch of four 720Bs triggered additional Lufthansa jet service to Africa. Twice-weekly flights began March 4 from Frankfurt to Lagos, continuing to Accra. At the end of the month, a twice-weekly flight was added from Frankfurt to Dakar via either Zurich or Paris. In addition, the Tehran service was expanded to include stops at Athens, Istanbul, Ankara and Beirut, starting April 2.

Lufthansa supplemented its North America flying with 720Bs. The summer 1962 schedule shows thrice-weekly Frankfurt–Shannon–New York service beginning May 1, plus a weekly San Francisco flight from Frankfurt via Paris and Montreal on May 5. African flying was enhanced on May 14 with the addition of new twice-a-week service from Frankfurt to Johannesburg via Athens, Khartoum and Nairobi.

The longest flying undertaken by Lufthansa's 720Bs was on the Far East route as an extension of Middle East schedules. With the pulldown of seasonal, 720B North American flying, the type took over from the 707 with a three-times-a-week Tokyo service from Frankfurt on October 3. Each flight called on six or seven cities en route, varying by day of the week. Intermediate destinations were Munich, Rome, Cairo, Dhahran, Karachi, Calcutta, Bangkok and Hong Kong. Eastbound, the marathon flights would leave at 10:15 a.m. from Frankfurt and arrive at Tokyo the following evening. Portions of the route were operated as part of a pooling agreement with Alitalia and Pakistan International.

Daily Frankfurt–Vienna roundtrips were flown with the 720B from April 1, 1963. A day later, service to Spain began as part of the Lufthansa-Iberia pooling agreement. The 720Bs operated three days a week to Madrid and four times weekly to Barcelona, with all seven flights returning via Frankfurt to Dusseldorf. At the same time, the Tokyo service began originating from Dusseldorf, flying back to Frankfurt and resuming the balance of the Far East route.

Kuwait and New Delhi were added to the 720B schedules in July and September 1963, followed by Las Palmas in December, all on a weekly basis. Towards the end of its career with Lufthansa, the 720Bs began calling at Tripoli on April 5, 1964. Its final trans-Atlantic service, twice weekly from Frankfurt to Philadelphia via Boston, was initiated on April 3, 1965. Three days thereafter, a twice-weekly 720B service commenced from Frankfurt to Sydney via Athens, Karachi, Bangkok, Singapore and Darwin.

Lufthansa utilized its 720B fleet to the fullest, assigning the type to a variety of routes during a relatively short life with the carrier. (The Boeing Company Archives)

Lufthansa began disposing of its 720Bs after only three years, well ahead of the 707-430s. The airline took delivery of two turbofan-powered 707-330Bs in 1963, then acquired five more, plus a 707-330C by the end of 1965. These purchases more than equaled the six remaining 720Bs in the fleet; two had been lost in training accidents (see Chapter VI). In addition, new Boeing 727-30 tri-jets began arriving in March 1964 and took over some of the shorter 720B segments. All six 720-030Bs were sold to Pan American World Airways and left the fleet on a gradual basis. The first two were withdrawn in March 1964, followed by another at the end of that year. The fourth was handed over to Pan Am in December 1965, and the final two departed in January and February 1966.

Shiny and new with a bright red tail, N721US undergoes engine testing prior to delivery. It would spend 10 years with Northwest. (Museum of Flight/Gordon Williams Collection)

Northwest Airlines

Claimed to be the second oldest U.S. airline with a continuous name, Northwest Airlines (NWA) grew from a pioneering, seat-of-the-pants company in the 1920s to a global giant now dominant among the major American air carriers. More significantly, it has done so while operating in some of the most challenging weather regions in the country.

Northwest became the fourth coast-to-coast airline when it began flying a route from New York to Portland and Seattle/Tacoma in June 1945. Stopping at Detroit and Milwaukee, the service hopscotched across Minnesota, North Dakota, Montana and Washington to the West Coast. A year later, flights to Alaska commenced from Seattle/Tacoma to Anchorage in anticipation of new service to Japan that would begin in 1947. The airline also took up the marketing name Northwest Orient Airlines, which it would use for the next 40 years and then quietly drop.

From postwar DC-3 and DC-4 equipment, Northwest upgraded its fleet to include Martin 202 twins plus Boeing 377 Stratocruisers, then DC-6Bs, Lockheed 1049G Constellations and finally DC-7Cs. By the

Staged photos show Northwest's first-class and coach cabin interiors, no doubt utilizing Boeing employees and family members as "passengers." (The Boeing Company Archives)

	Northwest	
Registration	Fleet No.	msn
N721US	721	18351
N722US	722	18352
N723US	723	18353
N724US	724	18354
N725US	725	18355
N726US	726	18356
N727US	727	18420
N728US	728	18421
N729US	729	18422
N730US*	730	18381
N731US*	731	18382
N732US*	732	18383
N733US*	733	18384
N734US	734	18687
N735US	735	18688
N736US	736	18792
N737US	737	18793

*Originally leased to TWA

Northwest 720Bs emerged from the Renton factory even as Eastern's non-fan versions were still being produced. (Museum of Flight/Gordon Williams Collection)

N725US wears "Fan-Jet" titles on its forward fuselage in this April 1968 picture, taken at New York-JFK. (Harry Sievers)

mid-1950s, the company route map included Hawaii (served from Seattle/Tacoma and Portland) and segments beyond Tokyo to Okinawa, Manila, Taipei, Hong Kong and the Korean cities of Pusan and Seoul. Florida service from the Midwest was granted to NWA in 1958 as the industry approached the Jet Age.

For short- and medium-length flights, Northwest selected the Lockheed 188C Electra, announcing an order for 10 airplanes on May 1, 1958. Options for 18 more were secured a year later, although only eight were taken up. As its first turbine-powered equipment arrived, NWA planners put the type into service on September 1, 1959, over routes that varied from the New York–Milwaukee–Minneapolis/St. Paul run to the nonstop New York–Seattle/Tacoma service. Electras were an interim aircraft on the transcontinental segment, to be soon taken over by pure jets.

Northwest turned to Douglas for its initial long-haul jet needs, ordering five DC-8-32 intercontinental models on December 30, 1958. The type entered service between Seattle/Tacoma and Tokyo in July 1960. New York-Idlewild–Anchorage–Tokyo flights began in September, along with service west of Tokyo. Acquisition of all five aircraft by January 1961 allowed NWA to rapidly replace its piston-powered equipment on the highly profitable Orient flights.

To upgrade service on important domestic routes, Northwest's managers finally settled on the Boeing 720B after a year of negotiations. A $36.7-million order for six airplanes that included options for six more was announced on March 16, 1961. Original plans called for a 38-first-class and 69-tourist-class configuration. Boeing apparently counted on this transaction early on and began building the airplanes, as the first 720-051B

Seen in June 1973, N737US makes an appearance with only Northwest titles. It migrated to Maersk Air a year later. (Harry Sievers Collection)

was delivered only four months later, allowing a July 1, 1961 startup of service on the Minneapolis/St. Paul–New York-Idlewild route. The second aircraft quickly followed and was used for route-proving flights to Anchorage and Honolulu.

Although information on the options is sketchy, Boeing instead leased four airplanes built to Northwest's specifications to TWA that fall, then delivered them to NWA in late 1962.

Northwest found the 720B to be well-suited to its needs, and three options were converted to firm orders only a month after service startup. Domestic jet flights increased to points in Florida plus New York–Seattle/Tacoma nonstops, and West Coast–Hawaii service. All nine aircraft arrived by the end of 1961. The type's success prompted the airline's planners to acquire an all-Boeing fleet. In June 1962, it was formally announced that Northwest would purchase three long-range, 707-320B jetliners, along with two additional 720Bs, allowing a phase out of the DC-8s; one was sold off that year, along with the remaining four in 1963. By the end of 1962, 13 720Bs were in the fleet; one additional unit was delivered in 1963. Chicago–Anchorage–Tokyo flights utilized the type, along with Seattle/Tacoma–Anchorage service. Northwest began calling itself "the fan-jet airline" after its conversion to all-Boeing jets, claiming to have been first with all-turbofan-powered jets.

All of Northwest's trans-Pacific flights were jet-powered by May 1963, with 707-351Bs flying most of the longer segments and 720Bs continuing beyond Tokyo to Seoul, Okinawa, Taipei and Manila. Meanwhile, the JT3D-1 turbofan engines that powered the 720Bs were upgraded by Northwest technicians to the JT3D-3 configuration, increasing the power plant's thrust from 17,000 pounds to 18,000 pounds and allowing its use interchangeably on 707-351B and 720B models.

Domestically, the 720Bs fanned out to most of Northwest's major destinations. Three more units were acquired in 1964, bringing the total

number delivered to 17, although one had been lost in the February 12, 1963 accident (see chapter VI). Along with the last two 720Bs ordered in February 1964, Northwest signed for 11 Boeing 727-51s to use on shorter domestic flights. The first tri-jets were scheduled to arrive only a few months after the last 720Bs. Additional 707-351B and -351C variants came on-line, mainly for long-haul and military contract work.

As Northwest built up its jet fleet with more 727s during the mid-1960s, the 720B fleet still represented a major portion of the airline's flight schedule, particularly within the United States. By the end of 1968, all trans-Pacific service, including Hawaii, was flown by 707 equipment, with 720Bs serving 20 cities in the continental United States plus Anchorage and Winnipeg. Among the shortest segments was the Fargo, North Dakota–Minneapolis/St. Paul run, plus a few "tag-on" routes within Florida and between East Coast cities. Longer flights included Chicago–Seattle/Tacoma, Seattle/Tacoma–Anchorage and trans-continental nonstops between Seattle/Tacoma and both Washington-Dulles and New York-JFK.

Northwest's acquisition of Boeing 747s made some of its older aircraft redundant. The jumbos began arriving in 1970, followed only three years later by DC-10-40s. While the 720Bs were among NWA's most expensive jets to operate, the type was still relatively young with considerable market value, making it the logical candidate for retirement, even ahead of some larger-capacity 707s. Beginning in late 1971, the fleet was gradually withdrawn and sold off, with the final two aircraft departing in early 1974. A single unit was bought by the Taiwan government, but the remaining 15 airplanes went to only three buyers. Olympic Airways of Greece took seven, and the remaining eight were split evenly between two charter operators, Monarch Airlines and Maersk Air. During 13 years with Northwest, the 720B proved to be the right aircraft for a major role in the airline's growth and transition to jets.

Northwest's 720B fleet performed yeoman service on both domestic and international routes. (The Boeing Company Archives)

Pictured in Alaska, one of PNA's Constellations is flanked by N720W, the new queen of the fleet. (The Boeing Company Archives)

Pacific Northern Airlines

Woodley Airways was born on April 10, 1932. Arthur Woodley began flying his five-passenger Bellanca from Merril Field at Anchorage when the territory of Alaska was little more than a wilderness. The airline acquired Travelair planes in 1935 and added routes to Kodiak and Bristol Bay. Following World War II, Woodley became the first regularly scheduled air carrier in Alaska and, in 1945, changed its name to Pacific Northern Airlines (PNA). By then, it had begun flying multi-engine equipment in the form of two ex-military Boeing 247s. DC-3s were added a year later.

Stretching its wings, PNA began Anchorage–Seattle flights in 1950 and was authorized to fly to Fairbanks from Portland and Seattle in 1951. The new "lower 48" flights were operated with DC-4s and included Juneau–Seattle service, added in 1953. The airline would upgrade to Lockheed 749 and 749A Constellations by 1955. Kodiak and Ketchikan service was added as the route map continued to grow.

Still the company's chairman, Woodley floated an $11-million loan in 1961 to purchase two new Boeing 720-062 jetliners. The amount of the loan, equal to PNA's gross income for that same year, enabled startup of turbine service on April 27, 1962. The inaugural flight departed from Seattle at 8:45 a.m. and flew nonstop to Anchorage, covering the 1,450-mile segment in 2 hours and 52 minutes. Two days later, jet flights commenced between Seattle, Ketchikan and Juneau. At the time, PNA's fleet also included seven Constellations and three DC-3s.

The company 720s established a high rate of reliability and carried heavy passenger and cargo loads. The duo received wide publicity after the devastating "Good Friday" 1964 earthquake hit Anchorage, Seward and surrounding areas in Alaska. Mercy missions were flown around the clock, bringing in relief personnel and supplies while southbound flights carried injured and homeless back to Seattle. Those of other airlines, along with military aircraft joined the PNA 720s.

In 1965, the Civil Aeronautics Board realigned Alaska routes, which cost PNA its monopoly on the prime

Seattle–Anchorage segment. Northwest was granted authority on the route, and Pacific Northern's Portland authority was suspended. However, it did gain a lesser, monopoly segment between Ketchikan and Juneau. An ex-Aer Lingus 720-048 was purchased from Braniff a year later after an order for four new 727s had been canceled when PNA was unable to secure sufficient financing. Even though his airline was profitable and carrying more passengers to Alaska from Seattle than Alaska, Northwest and Pan Am combined, Woodley became discouraged when he could not expand his operation. Figuring that the day of the small airline was over, he began thinking about merging with a larger carrier.

After considering Braniff and Continental, Woodley began discussions with the management of Western Airlines. On October 1, 1967, Pacific Northern and Western formally merged, and the PNA name disappeared. The three 720s joined an enlarged Western fleet.

PNA Chairman Arthur Woodley (second from right) and airline managers pose after touring N720V, the airline's first jet. (The Boeing Company Archives)

	PNA	
Registration	**msn**	**Model**
N720V	18376	062
N720W	18377	062
N7081*	18042	048
*Purchased from Braniff		

Acquired used from Braniff, 720-048 N7081 was photographed at Seattle/Tacoma in January 1967, still wearing basic Braniff colors. (Harry Sievers)

One of two spacious galleys on PNA's 720s included an auxiliary table for meal tray preparation. The emergency escape slide ceiling compartment is also visible. (The Boeing Company Archives)

Another staged photo shows Pacific Northern's cockpit layout. (The Boeing Company Archives)

The 720's shorter fuselage length is readily apparent in this in-flight study of N720W. (The Boeing Company Archives)

PIA's first 720B, delivered on November 6, 1962, entered service between Karachi and London three months later. (The Boeing Company Archives)

Pakistan International Airlines – PIA

Pakistan's flag carrier was established in 1951 by the country's ministry of defense and began service with three Lockheed 1049C Constellations three years later, between Karachi and Dacca. Service was extended to London via Cairo, Rome and Geneva in 1955, and the airline was formally established as a civilian carrier, although still government owned. Pakistan International Airlines Corporation (PIA) then merged with Orient Airways, acquiring its smaller aircraft and domestic routes. Vickers Viscounts were added to modernize the fleet in 1959 along with Fokker F.27s in 1961.

PIA leased a Boeing 707-321 (N723PA) from Pan Am in 1960 to upgrade its Karachi–London route to pure-jet service beginning on March 7, 1960. Weekly London–New York service was added two months later. Approval for the airline to acquire three 720Bs was given by the Pakistan government in April 1961. The first 720-040B, AP-AMG, was

delivered on December 21, 1961, and entered service in February 1962 between Karachi and London. Initial jet flights operated twice weekly via Tehran, Geneva and Frankfurt; and twice weekly via Tehran, Beirut and Rome. In addition, Karachi–Dacca segments operated two days a week.

Service to New York from London was increased to twice weekly in April, with a third weekly service scheduled from May 1. The second and third 720Bs arrived in November, allowing increased jet service to Europe, the Middle East and later to East Pakistan, which later secured its independence as Bangladesh. The leased Pan Am 707 was returned at the end of 1962.

Disappointing trans-Atlantic loads prompted Pakistan International managers to cancel the London–New York service in March 1963; however, negotiations that year with the Russian government produced an agreement allowing PIA to add Moscow as an en route stop on its European service from May 1964, using 720Bs. The airline also received permission to provide

Pakistan International changed its color scheme slightly, as evidenced by this July 1976 picture, taken at Paris-Orly. (Airliners Collection)

PIA operated 720Bs for 24 years, well into the widebody jet era. (The Boeing Company Archives)

the first direct air service to Shanghai, capital city of the People's Republic of China, from a non-Communist country. Weekly Dacca–Canton (now Guangzhou)–Shanghai 720B service began on April 29, 1964.

Tragedy struck when AP-AMH, operating a new route on the Karachi–London service, crashed on May 20, 1965, while on approach to Cairo Airport, killing all 121 passengers (see Chapter VI). Just before the accident, when PIA's fourth and final factory-delivered 720B arrived, a 720-048 leased from Aer Lingus was returned.

Two Boeing 707-340C jetliners joined the fleet in 1966 to support expanded service. PIA began flying to nine new cities by year-end. Another pair of 707s would be acquired over the following two years with additional units bought and leased to form the bulk of the airline's jet equipment.

The 720B fleet remained at three until March 1974 when AP-AMJ was leased to Air Malta in conjunction with a management assistance program for that carrier. During the same month, PIA received its first of three DC-10-30s on order. Also in 1974, three 720-047Bs were bought from Western Airlines for additional capacity. The first, acquired for parts, was ferried to Karachi in July, then stripped of its components and scrapped. The second and third aircraft arrived in August and September and were pressed into service.

Even with two leased 747-200s joining PIA's fleet in 1976, a single 720-030B was bought from Alia Jordanian

Airlines during the year. Two additional 720-047Bs were purchased from Western in September 1978. Finally, a 720-027 served briefly with PIA on lease during the last four months of 1978, bringing the total number of 720s to fly with the airline up to 12. Only a year later, one of the original factory-delivered aircraft, AP-AMG, was sold to Air Malta.

As PIA continued to upgrade its fleet, the 720Bs were gradually phased out. AP-AXK, damaged in a landing accident on January 8, 1981, was not repaired. Two more aircraft were retired that year including AP-AZP, which was preserved. A single 720B was withdrawn in 1985, and the last two soldiered on until 1986, closing out 24 years of service with PIA.

Pakistan International			
Registration	msn	Model	Notes
AP-AMG	18378	040B	
AP-AMH	18379	040B	
AP-AMJ	18380	040B	
AP-ATQ	18745	040B	
EI-ALC	18043	048	Leased from Aer Lingus 10/64–4/65
AP-AXQ	18062	047B	Purchased from Western
AP-AZP	18250	030B	Purchased from Alia
N733T	18581	027	Sub-leased from Aeroamerica
AP-BAF	18589	047B	Purchased from Western
AP-AXK	18590	047B	Purchased from Western
AP-AXM	18749	047B	Purchased from Western
AP-AXL	18818	047B	Purchased from Western

AP-ATQ wears PIA's final 720B livery update, photographed in December 1984. (Choice Aviation Photo/Stefano Pagiola Collection)

TWA provided pilot training for SDI; hence, the company's ground power unit is visible in this photo taken at Kansas City's Mid-Continent Airport. Seen in its delivery scheme, HZ-ACB entered service in March 1962. (Museum of Flight/Gordon Williams Collection)

Saudi Arabian Airlines

Directed by Saudi Arabian officials with technical assistance from Trans World Airlines, Saudi Arabian Airlines (SDI) commenced domestic operations in 1946 with a trio of DC-3s. One of them had been earlier received as a gift from U.S. President Franklin D. Roosevelt to King Abdulaziz Bin Abdulrahman Al Saud. From that humble beginning, the airline has grown to rank among the world's top international carriers with worldwide routes.

By 1960, SDI was operating passenger flights with DC-3, DC-4 and Convair 340 equipment within the Kingdom and to a few neighboring Middle Eastern countries. The airline's managers took advantage of two early delivery positions and ordered a pair of 720Bs in September 1961. The opportunity came when Ethiopian Airlines delayed its order while awaiting completion of the new airport at Addis Ababa.

The two 720-068Bs were handed over in December, only three months after being ordered, and were initially used for crew training. Regular passenger service commenced on March 15, 1962, between Jeddah and Beirut. Flights to Riyadh, Dhahran and Cairo quickly followed. Service was extended to Karachi and Bombay in 1965. Then, in 1967, Saudi Arabian's 720Bs opened a new route to London via Beirut, Geneva and Frankfurt. The arrival of three Douglas DC-9-15s that year freed up the 720Bs for the longer routes.

In 1966, two 707-368C inter-continental jets arrived and, for the most part, replaced the 720Bs on the airline's longest routes, although the latter remained compatible with the new Boeings. At the same time, London service was upgraded when nonstop flights from the Kingdom were introduced, and new Jeddah–Rome nonstops commenced.

The DC-9s were sold in 1972, replaced by Boeing 737-200s; eventually, 18 737-268s and two convertible 737-268C variants replaced the Douglas jets and remaining non-turbine equipment. During that year, the airline adopted a new color scheme and took the shortened "Saudia" as its corporate identity.

The 720Bs remained even as additional intercontinental 707s were acquired. Retention of the older jets was necessary in order to keep up with the airline's rapid growth. Lockheed L-1011 TriStars began arriving in 1975. A 720-024B was leased from Ethiopian Airlines from March 1975 until February 1976, when two 720Bs were leased for a year from Middle East Airlines.

The original jet livery was replaced in 1964 with SDI's more traditional scheme that earlier appeared on its piston-powered equipment. Saudair titles were worn in the early to mid-1960s. HZ-ACB was photographed on approach to Kansas City International Airport in 1965, while back in the United States for heavy maintenance. (Bob Woodling)

HZ-ACB wears full Saudi Arabian titles in this picture taken at London-Heathrow in May 1967. (Harry Sievers)

In 1977, Saudia leased two MEA 747-2B4B jumbos for increased lift on its Riyadh–London routes and a daily Riyadh–Cairo–Jeddah roundtrip, plus a weekly service between Riyadh and Beirut. By then, SDI owned a 707 fleet that had grown to nine with additional aircraft leased from several carriers. Two 720s were leased briefly from Aeroamerica, probably for Haj pilgrimage flights, and did not wear SDI colors.

As new-aircraft deliveries began to catch up with capacity growth, the two 720Bs were finally retired in July 1979 and stored briefly at Jeddah. Both were sold to Overseas International Distributors and ferried to the United States. Although one aircraft was used briefly for experimental research, neither of them carried passengers again. Both shared the distinction of serving entire careers with one airline.

Saudi Arabian			
Registration	msn	Model	Notes
HZ-ACA	18165	068B	
HZ-ACB	18166	068B	
ET-AFK	18417	024B	Leased from Ethiopian
N733T	18581	027	Leased from Aeroamerica
N736T	18064	027	Leased from Aeroamerica
OD-AGF	18830	047B	Leased from MEA
OD-AFR	18018	023B	Leased from MEA

The last color scheme worn by Saudia's 720Bs is seen on ET-AFK, an ex-Continental -024B variant leased from Ethiopian for one year in 1975-76. (Airliners Collection)

One of Western's later-delivered 720Bs receives pre-delivery attention on the Renton ramp. This revised Indian-head livery debuted with the airline on the 720B. (The Boeing Company Archives)

Western Airlines

Advertised as "America's Oldest Airline," Western was formed as Western Air Express in 1925 and flew its first service a year later with a Douglas M-2 mail plane. Operating in the western United States, the fledgling airline would in 1932 gain the distinction of operating the first four-engine commercial land plane in the United States, Fokker's 32-passenger F-32.

The company's name was officially changed to Western Air Lines (WAL) in 1941. By this time, its relationship with Boeing was limited to a few, used model 247s, purchased and acquired as the result of smaller airline acquisitions. Douglas would supply DC-3s, then DC-4s and DC-6Bs as the carrier built up its route structure, with Convair 240s replacing the DC-3s on the airline's short- and medium-haul segments.

Western became a prominent operator along the West Coast and over its mountain routes from Los Angeles to Edmonton and Minneapolis/St. Paul. Famous for its "Champagne" and "Hunt Breakfast" flights, the airline maintained high standards of in-flight service and aircraft appearance. By the mid-1950s, it adopted the "Western Airlines" name and introduced an attractive new color scheme that featured an Indian head logo. Service to Mexico City was initiated in 1957, a year

after Western ordered nine Lockheed model 188 Electra turboprop aircraft. The type was considered ideally suited to WAL's route structure, which contained no segments in excess of 1,000 miles except for the 1,550-mile Los Angeles–Mexico City route. Even though some Western managers wanted to order pure jets, Terry Drinkwater, Western's president, refused to do so, reasoning that the Electra could do the job just

Western President Terrell C. Drinkwater (brown suit and bow tie) and Boeing President William Allen (fourth from right) are joined by other airline and Boeing officials at Western's first 720B delivery ceremony. (The Boeing Company Archives)

Western			
Registration	**Fleet No.**	**msn**	**Model**
N93141	341	18061	047B
N93142	342	18062	047B
N93143	343	18063	047B
N93144	344	18167	047B
N93145	345	18451	047B
N93146	346	18452	047B
N93147	347	18453	047B
N93148	348	18588	047B
N93149	349	18589	047B
N93150	350	18590	047B
N93151	351	18749	047B
N93152	352	18818	047B
N93153	353	18820	047B
N3154	354	18827	047B
N3155	355	18828	047B
N3156	356	18829	047B
N3157	357	18830	047B
N3158	358	18963	047B
N3159	359	19160	047B
N3160	360	19161	047B
N3161	361	19207	047B
N3162	362	19208	047B
N3163	363	19413	047B
N3164	364	19414	047B
N3165	365	19438	047B
N3166	366	19439	047B
N3167	367	19523	047B
N720V*	301	18376	062
N720W*	302	18377	062
N7081*	303	18042	048

*acquired via PNA merger

Western contracted with Boeing to perform modifications and improvements to its 720B fleet. One of the aircraft undergoes crown skin replacement in 1969. (The Boeing Company Archives)

as well. When pressed on the subject, his candid reply was, "Would you buy the *Queen Mary* to sail across Lake Tahoe?" However, the picture changed when Western applied for routes between the U.S. mainland and Hawaii as part of the Trans-Pacific Route Case. With no way of knowing when the routes might be approved, Drinkwater caved in and ordered three Boeing 720s in February 1960 for delivery beginning in April 1961. Also announced was an option for a fourth aircraft plus five more options dependent on receiving the Hawaii route authority.

Once again, the Convair 880 was under serious consideration but lost out to Boeing. One of the factors that may have swayed the decision was the availability of two 707-139s, which Western agreed to lease. The pair had been built for Cuba's national airline, Cubana de Aviacion, but not taken up, and the availability of these jets for a June 1960 startup gave Western the ability to begin Hawaii service almost immediately, should it receive authority to do so on short notice.

Western inaugurated its 707 service on June 1, 1960, with three daily roundtrips between Los Angeles and Seattle/Tacoma. One flight operated nonstop, another flew via San Francisco and the third via Portland. These trips replaced Electras that had been in service since August 1959. The turboprops replaced some DC-6B flying, allowing further withdrawal of Convair 240s; the last would be retired in February 1961.

The single 720 option was taken up only a month after the 707s entered service. The June 7, 1960 announcement contained the first reference to the fact that Western had opted for turbofan-powered 720Bs rather than originally specified 720s.

Delivery of the first 720-047B to Western came on April 7, 1961, followed closely by the remaining three aircraft in May, June and August, respectively. Touted as "Western's new 640-mph Fan/Jets – The fastest takeoff, climb and cruise this side of sound," the type entered service on May 15 between Los Angeles and Mexico City, and was extended north to San Francisco and Seattle/Tacoma on June 1. The 720Bs completely replaced the 707s on West Coast segments by June 16. With Hawaii route authority still in limbo, the larger Boeings were re-deployed to Western's mountain route between San Francisco and Minneapolis/St. Paul via Denver, plus Los Angeles-Minneapolis/St. Paul via Salt Lake City. The first four aircraft were delivered with seating for 40 first-class and 74 coach passengers.

Three more 720Bs were ordered in October 1961 for delivery in July and August 1962, which allowed the return of the 707-139s to Boeing. The additional capacity upgraded some flights operated by the Electras, allowing route expansion and a continued decline in DC-6B flying. Although Hawaii authority from San Diego and Los Angeles was given to Western in early 1961, the CAB attached a temporary stay order to its decision that prevented service startup.

Nevertheless, the airline continued to purchase 720Bs. A contract for three more was announced in January 1963 with deliveries scheduled in April, May and June of the following year.

Western's managers made a significant decision in 1964. Rather than order Boeing 727s, they decided to standardize on only two fleet aircraft, the Electra and 720B, reasoning that the savings realized by the 727's better fit on some routes would be offset by costs of introducing and maintaining a third type. Accordingly, four more 720Bs were purchased for delivery in spring 1965, to boost the fleet total to 17. The remaining 14 DC-6Bs were almost fully depreciated and planned for retirement as the new

One of three 720s acquired from PNA, N720V makes at appearance at Los Angeles International in December 1971, wearing full Western colors. (Harry Sievers Collection)

Boeings arrived. It was assumed that smaller jets would replace the Electras, but the type continued with Western until the early 1970s. Meanwhile, the 720B's cruising speed was reduced from mach 0.86 to mach 0.84, realizing a 4% to 5% savings in fuel costs.

By mid-1964, 720B service had been expanded to include Los Angeles–Sacramento plus a route from San Diego to Minneapolis/St. Paul via Phoenix and Denver. In September, United began 727 "Jet Commuter" flights between Los Angeles and San Francisco with a $14.50 one-way fare in response to PSA's $13.50 Electra service. Western countered with DC-6B "Thriftair" flights, offering a rock-bottom tariff of $11.43 ($12, including tax). United turned up the heat with 14 daily, roundtrip Jet Commuter flights, causing WAL to cut back on its DC-6B service until

1965. Then, three factory-fresh 720Bs configured with all-coach seating for 146 passengers, formed WAL's new "FANJET COMMUTER" service between Los Angeles and San Francisco, matching United's $13.50 fare. These commuter flights were later extended from Los Angeles to Las Vegas as well. The 720Bs were now being touted as "the jet with the extra engine," a claim based on the extra power of its turbofan engines that equaled five conventional turbojets.

Western would acquire another 10 720Bs, making it the largest purchaser of the type, with one additional delivery in 1965, then four in 1966 and five in 1967, for a total of 27. The more generous first-class seating was reduced, initially to 28 with 92 in coach, then to 24 first-class and 98 coach. New service to Acapulco began in 1965, nonstop from

"Flying W" colors first appeared on Western's 720Bs in 1970. N3154, one of the first to be repainted, looks immaculate at Columbus, Ohio in December of that year, where it was about to depart on a charter flight to the Rose Bowl football game in California. (Harry Sievers)

Los Angeles and via San Diego and Mexico City, followed by Los Angeles–Minneapolis/St. Paul nonstops a year later, along with new flights to Vancouver, British Columbia.

As mentioned earlier, Pacific Northern Airlines was merged into the Western route system on July 1, 1967. PNA's three turbojet 720s joined the fleet and maintained schedules between Seattle and Alaska before flying through to Portland and California. Four Western Electras, converted to passenger-cargo configurations, would take over PNA's Constellation flying. Three additional turboprops were modified to all-cargo layouts, also for Alaska flying.

Five long-range 707-347Cs were acquired in mid-1997, as Western's quest for Hawaii route authority seemed imminent, although the airline's final 720B delivery – also the last 720 built – actually came a day after the fifth 707 was received. A substantial fleet of short-range 737-247s began arriving in mid-1968 as WAL continued to grow its route map and retire the last of the DC-6Bs plus the PNA-inherited Constellations.

Hawaii service was finally approved and began in July 1969, initially utilizing the 707 fleet. Competition for passengers on its new Pacific route was intense, in part because other carriers were also awarded similar new authority, but WAL captured a respectable 20% of the California–Hawaii traffic. An employee strike resulted in the decision to cancel orders for 12 Boeing jets including three 747s. To compete against the other airlines' soon-to-arrive jumbos, Western increased its seat pitch in coach and economy from 34 inches to 38 inches and added in-flight movies.

In 1970, six 720Bs were modified to "H" models, an internal designation and assigned to the "islander" fleet, as Hawaii frequencies were expanded. Navigators served on the 720Bs until cockpit crews were checked out on Doppler navigation systems. Ironically, initial passenger dissatisfaction with the 747s contributed to WAL's prosperity with narrowbody equipment.

Boeing 727-247 tri-jets were added to Western's fleet starting in late 1969 as well. Better suited for many of the company's routes, the type would eventually replace 720Bs on many segments. One 720B was sold to AVIANCA in September 1969, but continued airline growth delayed further retirement for a few years. Another 720B crashed during a crew training flight in March 1971 (see Chapter V).

A Western 720B was involved in a rather strange hijacking when, on June 2, 1972, a man took over a company 727 flight en route from San Francisco to Seattle and demanded cash, parachutes and transportation to Algeria. Negotiators were able to convince the fugitive to return to San Francisco from Seattle and switch to the longer-range 720H model that had been hastily flown in from Las Vegas.

N3164 then proceeded to New York's Kennedy Airport, where the remaining passengers were released. After a navigator boarded, the refueled aircraft flew 3,614 miles nonstop to Algiers. Stopping at Madrid on the way back to the United States, the aircraft was refueled for the first time since leaving New York, a total distance of 4,064 miles.

McDonnell Douglas DC-10-10 equipment joined Western in 1973 and was initially deployed on the Minneapolis/St. Paul–Los Angeles–Honolulu run. However, the widebody jets still shared Hawaii duties with the 707s and 720Bs. By this time, daily Anchorage–Honolulu flights were operating with 720Bs as well.

As with other operators, Western finally began to phase out older jet equipment when widebodies brought significant added capacity to the inventory. The three non-fan 720s were sold to Alaska Airlines in 1973. Seven 720Bs left in 1974, three to MEA and four to Pakistan International. After a three-year hiatus, two more 720Bs were bought by International Lease Finance Corporation (ILFC) in 1977 and leased to Eagle Air. The leasing company would buy three more of the type from Western during the next two years, for lease to different customers. An additional two went to MEA in 1978, plus a pair to private buyers in Saudi Arabia. The last

nine aircraft were sold in 1979, although the final unit was not delivered until January 1980. Six were bought by Wicklund Aviation, which resold one to the government of Togo, while the other five, acquired by the Boeing Military Aircraft Company for parts in conjunction with the KC-135E conversion program, were broken up at Davis-Monthan Air Force Base in Arizona.

A ceremony marking Western's final 720B revenue flight was held on September 14, 1979. But, as so often happens, the need for additional lift justified pulling an airplane out of retirement. N3162 went back into service in December and operated what turned out to be the final, final scheduled Western 720B flight, from Seattle/Tacoma to Los Angeles on January 6, 1980. The same airplane departed for good on January 25, nearly 19 years after Boeing 720Bs first arrived at Western's Los Angeles headquarters.

WESTERN AIRLINES

720B FAN JETS NOW LINK MAJOR CITIES OF CALIFORNIA – UTAH COLORADO – MINNESOTA

Fastest Flights between:
San Francisco—Denver . . . . 1 hr. 52 mins.
Denver—Minneapolis/St. Paul . . . . . 1 hr. 28 mins.
Minneapolis/St. Paul—Los Angeles . . 3 hrs. 28 mins.
Los Angeles—Salt Lake City . . . . 1 hr. 18 mins.

Chapter IV
SECONDARY OPERATORS

N734T in full Aeroamerica titles for service with the charter airline. Removed from service in 1980 at Seattle, the aircraft literally played one more role before its demise. (Stefano Pagiola Collection)

After leaving the service of the initial airline operators, most of the Boeing 720s continued to carry passengers for smaller carriers and travel clubs around the world. Some of the survivors were pressed into roles very different than envisioned by the manufacturer. These aircraft were converted to freighters, VIP aircraft and flying test beds.

Because so many of these aircraft changed owners several times, there were hundreds of different liveries, titles and registrations applied. This chapter is divided into four sections: Airlines; Travel Clubs & VIP Operators; Government & Private Owners; and Test Beds. Each section lists the participating operators in alphabetical order except when grouped under one parent company or for aesthetic reasons.

Aeroamerica		
Registration	msn	Model
N1776Q	18041	048
N302AS	18377	062
N303AS	18042	048
N7201U	17907	022
N7207U	17913	022
N7219U	18072	022
N730T	18154	027
N731T	18423	027
N733T	18581	027
N734T	18065	027
N736T	18064	027

Airlines
Aeroamerica

Organized in 1974 by Joel Eisenburg, Seattle-based Aeroamerica operated 11 Boeing 720s, plus a mix of 707 variants and even a DC-8 for a short period of time. The company was initially established as a charter operator and based a portion of its fleet in Berlin. However, scheduled service was begun in 1978 between Seattle/Tacoma and Spokane, followed by Seattle/Tacoma–Honolulu service.

The 720s wore a variety of different liveries and occasionally assumed the titles of other companies for subcontract work. Succumbing to financial problems, Aeroamerica lost its operating certificate in June 1980. Some of its charters operated later under Jet Set's certificate, but the company shut down for good in 1982. Six of the remaining 720s were later broken up at Boeing Field, Seattle.

Braniff International used N736T, then registered N7076, to inaugurate service from Houston to Chicago O'Hare via Dallas. Sold to Aeroamerica in 1973, it is shown parked at the main terminal of Boeing Field, Seattle, wearing the tan-and-red livery. Ownership of the aircraft remained with the charter airline until it was scrapped 10 years later. (Stefano Pagiola Collection)

Also purchased from Braniff (ex-N7080) in 1973, N730T last operated with Aeroamerica and was broken up in 1988. Sobel Air, Sudan Airways and Yugoslav Airlines leased the 720-027 between 1977 and 1979. (Airliners Collection)

N733T shows signs of the many operators that utilized the 720-027 over the years, with paint patches covering previous names and registrations. Sold by Braniff to American Aviation Services and immediately leased to Aeroamerica on October 9, 1973, it was later sub-leased to carriers in the Middle East, Africa and Asia. N733T is pictured at Miami in January 1979, less than one month before being placed in storage. It was later ferried to Boeing Field and scrapped. (Bruce Drum)

Aeroamerica leased N734T with Thunderbird titles to Caesars World Resorts. Small Aeroamerica titles can be seen just forward of the registration number. (Stefano Pagiola Collection)

N7207U taxis at Boeing Field, Seattle, in August 1978, wearing Aeroamerica's last livery. It featured striking Northwest Native American art on the tail and in the titles. Leased for 15 months from Eastern Aircraft Services, the aircraft was returned to the lessor in late 1979 and broken up in June 1983. (Bob Woodling)

No, it's not Paris-Orly, but Boeing Field. And the aircraft is not SAM 26000; but rather Aeroamerica's 720-027 N734T. ABC Circle Productions used it to simulate the arrival of Air Force One in Paris for a television film. The 1981 docudrama, "Jacqueline Bouvier Kennedy," starred James Franciscus and Jaclyn Smith (shown walking down the stairs). This was the final screen appearance for msn 18065. The aircraft was left derelict after filming and scrapped in 1984 at Boeing Field. (Museum of Flight/Gordon Williams Collection)

Aerocondor

Originally N7537A with American Airlines, 720-023B HK-1973 (msn 18023) was purchased in June 1972 by Aerocondor de Colombia. It is seen (above) at Miami in the airline's bright and distinctive livery. An updated color scheme appears on the same aircraft, stored in 1980. It was broken up at Miami in March 1981. Aerocondor also operated a second 720B, HK-1974 (msn 18028).

This ex-Northwest 720-051B was donated to struggling AERONICA – Aerolineas Nicaraguenses in February 1982 by Olympic Airways, and pressed into service on the Managua–Miami route. YN-BYI (msn 18688) would serve AERONICA for seven years. (Bryant Petitt Jr. Collection)

Aeromar

Dominican Republic-based Aeromar International operated charter and contract service flights from the late 1970s, using two 720s for passenger flights. Unable to launch scheduled service to U.S. destinations, the airline operation was liquidated in 1987.

Aeromar leased N7219U in June 1979 and re-registered it as HI-415. It was withdrawn from use in 1984 and stored. (Bruce Drum)

Above: Aeromar acquired N720CC (msn 17915) on lease in September 1979. Originally N7209U with United, the 720-022 still wears Reef Hotel markings from an earlier lease, along with Aeromar titles on the aft fuselage. (Al Rodriguez)
Below: Returned to a basic United livery to match its sister ship, HI-415, N720CC became HI-372 and was purchased off lease. It was broken up at Miami in 1987. (Thomas Livesey Collection)

Aerotal Colombia (Aerolineas Territoriales de Colombia) acquired a single 720-030B on lease in October 1980. HK-2558X (msn 18060), shown here at Bogota, was stored in July 1983 when the airline ceased operations and scrapped a year later. (Christian Volpati)

Santo Domingo-based Aerovias Quisqueyana leased and operated 720-022 N7207U for one month in mid-1977. Named *Duarte*, the aircraft carried Quisqueyana titles and Christopher Columbus' ship Santa Maria on the tail. (Bruce Drum)

Formed in the Dominican Republic, Hispaniola Airways began regular flights to Puerto Plata, Miami and New York in 1979, with Haiti service starting a year later. Acquired in 1982, 720-022 HI-401 (msn 18049) was withdrawn in 1984 and remains in poor condition at Puerto Plata. The airline went bankrupt in 1985. (Jon Proctor Collection)

Air Ceylon

Above: Air Ceylon leased ex-United 720-022 N64696 (msn 18013) from Atlas Aviation from December 1976 until August 1977. (Jon Proctor Collection)

Below: Shown in Air Ceylon full colors on the ramp at Colombo, former American 720-023B 4R-ACS joined the airline in March 1977 on a nine-month lease. Air Ceylon would cease operations in 1979 with the formation of a new national carrier, Air Lanka. (Terry Waddington Collection)

Established in 1973, Air Malta began operations a year later with two 720-040Bs leased (and later bought) from Pakistan International. Initial service began from Malta to London, Birmingham, Manchester, Rome, Frankfurt, Paris and Tripoli. Three 720-047B variants were acquired from Western during the next five years, with three more leased on short-term contracts. The last Air Malta 720B was retired in late 1989. 9H-AAK (msn 18063), one of the -047s from Western, is seen on rollout at Malta in May 1983. (Philippe Collet photo/Jon Proctor Collection)

Air Rhodesia

Salisbury-based Air Rhodesia acquired three 720-025s in April 1973.
Above: VP-YNM (msn 18242) served the airline until May 1983. Parted out, its fuselage was used as a cabin trainer at Harare.
(Harry Sievers Collection).
Below: Reflecting the changes in the Southern African country, Air Rhodesia became Air Zimbabwe Rhodesia in January 1980. Six months later, the name was shortened to Air Zimbabwe. VP-YNL (msn 18162) wears the name *Manicaland* on its nose. (Jon Proctor Collection)

African carrier Air Tanzania leased 720-022 N62215 (msn 18080) for two months beginning in December 1979. It wore basic Inair Panama colors with company titles. (Bob Woodling)

Alaska Airlines

After leasing a single Continental 720B briefly in 1972, Alaska purchased from Western the trio of non-fan 720s that airline had acquired when it merged with Pacific Northern. All three began flying Alaska's routes in spring 1973, from Seattle/Tacoma to Anchorage, Fairbanks, Juneau and Ketchikan. Each wore different color versions of a common scheme. In 1974, an ex-United 720 was acquired as well. Supplementing Alaska's 727s, the 720s were only considered an interim solution to capacity needs until more 727s could be added to the fleet. All four were withdrawn from service in fall 1975 and sold.

Still carrying the original Pacific Northern registration, 720-062 N720V (msn 18376) is towed to the departure gate at Seattle/Tacoma showing off its red and gold colors in June 1973. It would soon be re-registered N301AS. (Harry Sievers Collection)

Sister ship N720W (msn 18377) also began life with PNA, so it was right at home in Alaska. Seen at Anchorage wearing blue and gold in July 1973, the 720-062 shortly became N302AS. (Harry Sievers Collection)

The third 720 from Western, msn 18042 originally flew with Aer Lingus as EI-ALB. An -048 variant, she became N7081 with PNA, Western and also Alaska for a short time before donning the N303AS registration. The airplane displays its purple-and-gold colors at Los Angeles in October 1974, where it arrived on a charter flight. (Airliners Collection)

Displaying United-era stripes and a stern-faced Alaska Airlines Eskimo on the tail, N304AS (msn 18049) actually belonged to Pan American by the time this picture was taken at Miami in January 1976. Traded in by Alaska for 727s in November 1975, all four 720s were later sold to other companies without ever being operated by Pan Am. (Airliners Collection)

Alia – Royal Jordanian Airlines, purchased two former Lufthansa and Pan American 720-030Bs in 1972. JY-ADS (msn 18250), named *City of Madaba* and later *City of Bethlehem,* served on routes in the Middle East and Europe, along with JY-ADT (msn 18251). ADS was sold to Pakistan International in 1976. (Ueli Klee)

Ariana Afghan Airlines purchased 720-030B N785PA (msn 18060) from Pan Am in April 1973 for use on European routes. Re-registered YA-HBA, it served the Kabul-based carrier for seven years. (H.J. Schröder photo/Harry Sievers Collection)

Belize Airways

Registered as a private company in November 1974, Belize Airways acquired five 720-022s from United for $1.5 million. Two, VP-HCM and -HCO, were fitted with 132 seats in an all-economy layout. The airline was not able to begin revenue flights until October 1977, when it initiated a daily roundtrip between Miami and Belize City. San Salvador and San Pedro Sula were served from Belize City on alternating days.

A third aircraft (VP-HCN) was outfitted to carry freight but without a main-deck cargo door. In addition, one 720 (N64696, msn 18073) was leased for nine months in 1979, and records indicated that VP-HCQ also served as a freighter. Although all five were painted, it is not certain that all of the owned aircraft actually entered service before the airline ceased operations in January 1980. The Belize fleet languished at Miami until all five aircraft were broken up in 1983.

Belize				
Registration	Fleet No.	msn	Model	Name
VP-HCM	BAL-005	18046	022	*Belmopan*
VP-HCN	BAL-001	18074	022 (F)	*Altun-ha*
VP-HCO	BAL-004	18045	022	*Belize City*
VP-HCP		17917	022	*Dangriga*
VP-HCQ		18076	022 (F)	*Xunantunich*
N64696*		18073	022 (F)	*Ambergias Caye*

* Leased March–December 1979

Resting at Miami's Tamiami Airport in July 1978, VP-HCM appears freshly painted in full Belize colors but with a bare-metal belly. Notice its fleet number, BAL-005, curiously posted on top of the vertical fin. (Bruce Drum)

Altun-Ha, missing parts, is seen in storage at Miami in March 1982, more than two years after the airline ceased operations. It was broken up one year later. (Stefano Pagiola Collection)

VP-HCO features a white belly in addition to "Boeing 707-720" titles on its engines. (Bruce Drum)

Retired by United in 1973 and stored for nearly three years in Miami, the former N7211U (msn 17917) awaits a new livery at Belize City. (Jon Proctor Collection)

VP-HCQ bakes in the sun prior to its Belize livery application. (Jon Proctor Collection)

Calair

German charter operator Calair acquired five ex-Eastern 720-025s from Boeing in 1970. The aircraft were repossessed after Calair ceased operations in March 1972.
Above: D-ACIQ (msn 18163) was photographed at Basel in April 1971.
Below: Also at Basel, D-ACIP (msn 18162), with a different tail livery, sits stored in March 1972. (both Harry Sievers Collection)

The first operator of ex-United N7220U (msn 18073) was Delta Air Transport (DAT) of Belgium. Acquired in May 1974 and later re-registered as OO-VGM, it kept all elements of United's livery, except titles, while with the Antwerp-based charter carrier. The 720-022 was sold again in November 1975, to Atlas Aircraft Corporation. (Stefano Pagiola Collection)

CONAIR of Scandinavia

Consolidated Aircraft Corporation, doing business as CONAIR of Scandinavia, was formed in 1964 to operate passenger and inclusive-tour flights to holiday destinations from Scandinavia to destinations in Southern Europe, the Mediterranean and Africa. The airline's first jet equipment consisted of five ex-Eastern Boeing 720-025s purchased used from Boeing; all were delivered between April and August 1971.

Although OY-DSR was scrapped as the result of a hard landing at Copenhagen in 1974, the remaining four 720s operated into the early 1980s and were replaced beginning in 1981 by five 720-051Bs. These original Northwest Airlines aircraft, obtained from Maersk Air, had earlier been modified with two additional over-wing exits for high-density seating.

CONAIR began acquiring Airbus A300 widebodies in the mid-1980s, and phased out its 720B fleet in 1987. Four went to the Boeing Military Aircraft Company for parts and the fifth was sold to Allied Signal.

	CONAIR	
Registration	**msn**	**Model**
OY-DSK	18157	025
OY-DSL	18159	025
OY-DSM	18161	025
OY-DSP	18241	025
OY-DSR	18243	025
OY-APU	18792	051B
OY-APV	18793	051B
OY-APW	18422	051B
OY-APY	18421	051B
OY-APZ	18384	051B

Wearing CONAIR's attractive colors, 720-025 OY-DSK climbs away in this August 1980 photo. Utilized until 1982, the aircraft was re-registered as N3124Z, stored at Luton Airport in the United Kingdom, and later broken up. (Thomas Livesey Collection)

Still in basic Maersk Air colors, 720-051B OY-APW wears the titles of its new owner in May 1981, shortly after changing hands. (Bryant Petitt Jr. Collection)

Ecuatoriana

Quito-based Compania Ecuatoriana de Aviacion reorganized in 1970 as Ecuatorian Airlines with the trade name Ecuatoriana. Flying routes to Cali, Panama and Miami to the north, plus a southward Santiago segment via Guayaquil and Lima, the airline acquired two 720Bs in 1975 and a third in 1977. Boeing 707s were added, along with a DC-10, allowing retirement of the smaller Boeings starting in April 1984. The last 720B left the fleet in February 1986.

Ecuatoriana			
Registration	msn	model	name
N780EC/HC-AZO/HC-BDP	18033	023B	*Imbabura*
HC-ACP	18036	023B	*Galapagos*
HC-AZQ	18037	023B	*Imbabura*

Formerly clad in subtle American and Pan Am liveries, Ecuatoriana's HC-AZP became a wild expression of modern aviation art. Named *Galapagos*, it also carried the Ecuadorian military registration FAE-8036 on its fin. The 720B was leased, together with HZ-AZQ, in January 1975. (Al Rodriguez photo/Phil Brooks Collection)

Above: Still in Pan Am colors but now with Ecuatoriana titles and new registration, N780EC was pressed into service on April 1, 1977.
Below: Registered as EC-AZO, msn 18033 was re-registered EC-BDP following conversion to a freighter that included a main-deck cargo door installation, rare for a 720 variant. It wears a colorful, multi-shade green livery in this December 1982 photo taken at Miami. (both Bruce Drum)

Another ex-American and Pan Am aircraft, HC-AZQ is somewhat more subdued in this rainbow color scheme. Pictured departing from Miami for Quito, the name *Imbabura* can be seen on the nose. (Bryant Petitt Jr.)

Inair – Internationacional de Aviacion

Painted in the red, white and blue of the Panamanian flag, cargo carrier Inair registered former United Air Lines 720-022 N7212U (msn 18044) as HP-685 in 1974. It was written off after a crash outside of Barranquilla, Colombia on April 22, 1976, then replaced by another 720 (msn 18073). (Harry Sievers Collection)

To be acquired from United Air Lines in 1973, Inair's livery and registration (HP-679) had been applied to msn 18080, but the aircraft was not taken up. The 720-022, registered N62215, is shown at Phoenix in August 1977, then owned by Universal Airways. The number 679 can be seen on the nose, a reminder of its anticipated Panamanian registration. Inair went out of business in 1987. (via Nicky Scherrer)

Eagle Air

A group of former employees from the bankrupt charter airline Air Viking formed Eagle Air Arnarflug at Teykjavik, Iceland in April 1976. Initially operating charter flights to warm-weather European and Mediterranean destinations, the airline was authorized to provide scheduled domestic services in 1980. International destinations were also approved a year later. Three former Air Viking 720s went to Eagle Air for continuation of charter flights, but two were withdraw in 1976, followed by the third two years later. A pair of leased 720-047Bs joined the fleet in 1977 to perform both charter and scheduled flights. As the airline bought younger jets, these original Western aircraft were returned to the leasing company.

Eagle Air		
Registration	msn	Model
TF-VVB	18075	022
TF-VVA	18082	022
TF-VLA	18163	025
TF-VLC	18820	047B
TF-VLB	18827	047B

TF-VLA appears in Eagle Air's attractive colors at Dusseldorf in October 1976. Arnarflug, the airline's name in Icelandic, appeared in titles on the vertical fin. (Pete Jary)

Before migrating to Eagle Air, TF-VVA flew for Air Viking in basic United colors with company titles and crest. It is seen at London-Heathrow in November 1975. (Airliners Collection)

Eagle Air's two 720Bs were sub-leased to other carriers several times. Flanked by a TAE DC-8, TF-VLB prepares to depart from Dusseldorf in July 1978, shortly after returning from a stint with Air Malta, hence the hybrid livery. (Erik Bernhard Collection)

720-023B G-BGBA (msn 18014) was one of two leased from American Airlines by U.K. charter operator Invicta International, which chiefly operated Vickers Vanguards. The former N7528A is believed to be the only one to receive full Invicta colors. It was photographed in late 1974, shortly before the end of its lease period. (Erik Bernhard Collection)

Although Iraqi Airways canceled a 1962 order for two new Boeing 720Bs, the Baghdad-based carrier leased a 720-051B (msn 18381) from Monarch Airlines for three months in 1974. Retaining its U.K. registry, G-AZFB is serviced between flights at London-Heathrow in October of that year. (Erik Bernhard Collection)

Operating under the trade name Jet 24, Jet Charter Service acquired three 720-051Bs from Monarch in spring 1983 but only retained the aircraft until that summer, when they were sold to the Boeing Military Aircraft Company for use in the KC-135 upgrade program. N2464K (msn 18382), along with another Jet 24 Boeing, is seen parked at Miami in May 1983. (Bruce Drum)

In freighter configuration, but without a main-deck cargo door, N419MA (msn 18082) spent its last years owned by Jet Power, Inc., which operated the 720-022 on behalf of Air India. The Indian government impounded and stored the aircraft at Bombay in 1979, where it was eventually scrapped. (Terry Waddington Collection)

Kenya Airways leased and later purchased former Western Airlines 720-047B N93148 (msn 18588) for use on its routes to and from East Africa. Received on May 18, 1978, 5Y-BBX served the African airline until June 1989. Stored until 1992, its wings and tail were then removed; the fuselage served as a ground trainer at Nairobi. A second 720B was sub-leased for a short time by Kenya Airways in 1978. (Bryant Petitt Jr. Collection)

The first of two ex-Eastern 720s purchased by Korean Air Lines, HL-7402 (msn 18160), delivered in August 1969, is shown at Hong Kong just four months later. Korean Air received 10 years of flying service for its investment, and later it used the static aircraft for emergency and cabin training. (Harry Sievers)

Libyan Arab Airlines leased OD-AFW (msn 18026) from MEA between January 1976 and October 1977. The 720-023B was painted in the line's impressive, gold-and-white livery but retained its Lebanese registration throughout the lease period. (Stefano Pagiola Collection)

Maersk Air

Supplementing and eventually replacing its Fokker F.27 fleet, European charter operator Maersk Air purchased three 720-051Bs from Northwest in late 1972, and added two more in 1974. The turbofan-powered jets operated chiefly to Mediterranean sun points on behalf of Scandinavian inclusive-tour promoters. Replaced by Boeing 737s, the five 720Bs migrated to CONAIR in 1981, one of them via Britannia.

Above: The Maersk Air powder blue, solid-color livery is displayed on OY-APZ at Copenhagen airport in 1973. (Harry Sievers Collection)

Below: OY-APW wears Maersk's later color scheme in this 1977 photo. (Terry Waddington Collection)

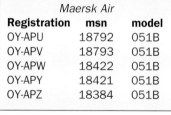

Maersk Air		
Registration	**msn**	**model**
OY-APU	18792	051B
OY-APV	18793	051B
OY-APW	18422	051B
OY-APY	18421	051B
OY-APZ	18384	051B

Middle East Airlines' OD-AFS taxis for departure at Beirut in July 1977. (Jon Proctor)

Middle East Airlines

Founded in 1945, Middle East Airlines (MEA) operated 21 Boeing 720Bs during a nearly 30-year period. During this time, it suffered the indignity of losing 11 of them to terrorism.

The Lebanese carrier started out with a modest route system to neighboring countries in the Middle East. After initiating flights to West Africa and Paris in 1954, it further expanded a year later to four more European destinations. In addition, Pakistan and India flights were added.

Having operated a mixed bag of turboprop and pure-jet types from the early 1960s, MEA gained its first experience with the 720 when three -060Bs were leased from Ethiopian Airlines in 1966 on a short-term basis, in anticipation of a contract to purchase new McDonnell Douglas DC-8-62s. When the order fell through because of financing problems, MEA extended the 720B leases and ordered four new Boeing 707-320Cs. One of the Ethiopian 720Bs was damaged beyond economical repair at Beirut on January 9, 1968; the other two were later returned to Ethiopian.

On December 28, 1968, an Israeli commando team attacked Beirut International Airport and blew up 13 airliners including eight of the MEA fleet. Destroyed were three Comet 4Cs, one of the two newly delivered 707s, a VC10, two Caravelles and a Viscount 700.

Several jets were acquired on short leases to cover for the lost aircraft while MEA looked for permanent replacements. A lease-purchase agreement with American Airlines was completed in June 1969 to acquire six of American's surplus Convair 990A jetliners, which MEA would use to standardize its fleet. Five were delivered that year, along with the second pair of 707-320Cs. The sixth 990A was received in January 1970.

Pleased with the 707s, MEA managers decided to concentrate on Boeing equipment as they continued the airline's equipment modernization program. Less than a year after delivering them, American Airlines agreed to take back the six Convair jets as partial payment for nine 720-023Bs. This transaction also allowed MEA to retire its last remaining Comet and Caravelle variants.

The first three MEA-owned 720Bs were handed over before the end of 1970, with the remaining six deliveries spread out over the following 13 months. Four more ex-American variants were purchased, with the last arriving in May 1973.

Turning to Western Airlines, MEA picked up three 720-047Bs in 1974, building its 720B fleet to 16. During the same year, two Boeing 747 Combi aircraft were delivered to MEA, which continued to expand. A third jumbo arrived in 1975.

While on lease from Ethiopian between January 1966 and March 1968, ET-AAH retained its Ethiopian cheatline painted in red, while titles of both airlines were retained. The 720-060B is seen at Rome in June 1966. (Harry Sievers)

OD-AFL was the first 720-023B received from American Airlines in 1970. The MEA initials were centered on the fuselage in this original livery, with the registration just forward of the horizontal stabilizer. The aircraft was written off in an attack at Beirut on August 21, 1985.
(Harry Sievers Collection)

OD-AFO poses at London-Heathrow in the second livery variation, with the registration moved to the vertical fin and fuselage titles relocated just behind the forward boarding door. The MEA initials were later brought a bit closer together, as seen on the opposite page in the top picture. Exiled to friendly countries during wartime, "Fox Oscar" returned to Lebanon only to be destroyed by gunfire on June 16, 1983. (Terry Waddington Collection)

OD-AGB was photographed in December 1988 at Geneva, showing off its attractive new and final livery. It provided the Lebanese airline with more than 22 years of service before being sold in 1995. (Jean-Luc Altherr photo/Stefano Pagiola Collection)

A bomb explosion aboard OD-AFT on January 1, 1976, killed all 81 passengers and crew. The aircraft was at 37,000 feet over Al Qaysumah, Saudi Arabia when the detonation occurred in the forward cargo compartment. (Terry Waddington Collection)

Beirut Airport remained closed for five months following the shelling of OD-AGE on June 27, 1976. (Airliners Collection)

In 1975, unrest in Lebanon escalated into a civil war. On New Year's Day 1976, 720B OD-AFT crashed during a flight from Beirut to Dubai, the victim of a terrorist bomb (see Chapter VI). After suspending operations for 17 days in June, MEA was returning to normal. Then, on June 27, warring factions shelling Beirut Airport inadvertently hit 720B OD-AGE instead of military aircraft on the field. The flight crew was still in the cockpit when the shell struck the port side wing root, causing a fuel tank explosion that instantly killed the captain. The first officer and flight engineer managed to escape through a cockpit window. Both were badly burned, and the first officer later died from his injuries. The aircraft was a total loss. Following this incident, the airport remained closed for nearly five months. Fearing for the safety of their employees, MEA managers temporarily moved the airline's base of operations to Paris in July. Charter and contract flying kept the fleet in the air, bringing in enough revenue to keep the airline afloat.

Two additional 720Bs were acquired from Western Airlines to replace the lost aircraft. By the end of 1976, Beirut Airport was again open for business and the airline resumed its regular schedule, albeit on a reduced basis. But civil unrest took its toll again in August 1981, when a dynamite explosion destroyed OD-AFR at the airport shortly after its arrival from Libya. During June 1982, Israeli warplanes destroyed four more 720Bs and two 707s at Beirut, with another 720B lost in August. Once again, the airport was closed, this time for 115 days. Finally, in August 1985, soon after the hijacking of a TWA 727 was resolved at Beirut, shelling destroyed one 720B and damaged a second beyond economical repair.

Although the destruction of MEA aircraft finally subsided, the airline was forced to endure sporadic operations for the rest of the 1980s. One 720B was sold in 1984 and another in 1986.

By early 1991, the type was retired from regular service, although equipment substitutions and crew-training flights continued. Another 720B was sold off in May, leaving only four still in MEA's inventory. Yet in June 1994, two aircraft – OD-AFM and -AGB – were pressed back into scheduled service for the busy summer season, restricted to use outside of Europe because they lacked hush kits. OD-AFZ had been broken up earlier that year, with -AGF serving as a source of spare parts.

The two reinstated aircraft, again stored in the fall, finally left Beirut for good in December 1995, sold to Pratt & Whitney Canada. Thus came to an end a long and sometimes violent relationship between MEA and the 720.

Middle East Airlines			
Registration	msn	Model	Notes
ET-AAG	18454	060B	Leased from Ethiopian
ET-AAH	18454	060B	Leased from Ethiopian
ET-ABP	18977	060B	Leased from Ethiopian
OD-AFL	18034	023B	Destroyed at Beirut 8/21/85
OD-AFM	18027	023B	
OD-AFN	18030	023B	
OD-AFO	18035	023B	Damaged beyond repair at Beirut 6/1/83
OD-AFP	18017	023B	Destroyed at Beirut 6/12/82
OD-AFQ	18024	023B	
OD-AFR	18018	023B	Destroyed at Beirut 8/31/81
OD-AFS	18019	023B	
OD-AFT	18020	023B	Destroyed in flight 1/1/76
OD-AFU	18029	023B	Destroyed at Beirut 6/16/82
OD-AFW	18026	023B	Destroyed at Beirut 6/16/82
OD-AFZ	18025	023B	
OD-AGB	18021	023B	
OD-AGE	18963	047B	Destroyed at Beirut 6/27/76
OD-AGF	18830	047B	
OD-AGG	18828	047B	Destroyed at Beirut 8/1/82
OD-AGQ	19160	047B	Destroyed at Beirut 8/21/85
OD-AGR	19161	047B	Destroyed at Beirut 6/16/82

Shaded lines indicate aircraft lost due to terrorism or military attack

Its thrust reversers engaged upon landing at Milan in November 1973, OD-AFR saw nearly 10 years of service with Middle East Airlines. The 720-023B survived civil war and invasion, only to be destroyed by a bomb at Beirut on August 31, 1981.
(Terry Waddington Collection)

MEA acquired N7540A from American Airlines on March 31, 1972. Re-registered OD-AFW, the aircraft was briefly leased to Nigeria Airways and Libyan Arab Airlines in the mid-1970s. Badly damaged by an attack on Beirut Airport on June 16, 1982, it was written off and scrapped.
(Airliners Collection)

One of the fortunate 720Bs, OD-AFM managed to survive the many conflicts that damaged or destroyed so many of her sister ships. After 25 years with MEA, the aircraft was retired and sold to Pratt & Whitney Canada in 1995 for use as spares.
(Stefano Pagiola Collection)

Maof

Short-lived Maof Airlines was formed in 1981 at Tel Aviv, a subsidiary of the Maof Group that owned two travel agencies. Along with a pair of 707s, it flew two 720Bs acquired from Monarch Airlines until declaring bankruptcy in 1984.
Above: 720-023B 4X-BMA (msn 18014) was photographed at Basel, Switzerland in November 1981. (Nicky Scherrer photo/Jon Proctor Collection)
Below: Engine start completed, 4X-BMB (msn 18013) prepares to pull away from its gate at Paris-Orly in June 1983. Along with its sister ship, it was one of the few 720-023Bs to have a second overwing exit installed for high-density seating. (Christian Volpati)

During the 1970s, Monarch Airlines acquired five 720-051Bs to replace its Bristol Britannia fleet, and leased one unit during 1974-75. The inclusive-tour charter operator picked up a pair of 720-023Bs in the late 1970s as well. The type was gone from Monarch's fleet by 1983. G-BCBB is seen at Manchester in August 1979. (Bob Woodling Collection)

Each of Olympic's 720Bs received the name of a Greek estuary with SX-DBG known as *Axios River*. It is seen beginning its takeoff run at Rhodes in September 1972. (Harry Sievers Collection)

Olympic Airways

Greek shipping tycoon Aristotle Onassis established Olympic Airways in 1956 after purchasing sole rights to all Greek air-transport operations. In early 1957, the airline began flying with a mix of DC-3 and DC-4 equipment. European routes were opened later in the year with leased DC-6Bs. Four factory-fresh DC-6Bs took over in 1958-59, allowing expanded domestic flying as well, plus new service to Cairo.

Comet 4B service between London and Athens began in 1960, but trans-Atlantic flying did not begin until Olympic received its first three Boeing 707-384C intercontinental jets in spring 1966. A mixed fleet of six 707-384B and -384C variants was operating by 1969, allowing retirement of the older Comets. Six 727-284s were also placed into service.

Olympic turned to the secondhand jet market in 1972, purchasing seven Boeing 720-051Bs from Northwest. Six were in service by June, with the seventh delivered in January 1973. The type's availability enabled Olympic to continue expansion and phase out its older, piston-powered airliners. Two surplus Northwest 707-351Cs were also acquired in 1973.

The 720Bs provided reliable service throughout the 1970s, even as Olympic increased its 727 fleet and acquired new 737 twin-jets and 747 jumbos. With five Airbus A300s coming on line, the 720Bs were withdrawn from service in January 1980. SE-DBN was leased to Air Tanzania for 10 months and later donated to AERONICA (see page 65), and another was sold off. The remaining five found no customers and were eventually broken up at Athens.

		Olympic	
Registration	**msn**	**Model**	**Name**
SX-DBG	18352	051B	*Axios River*
SX-DBH	18353	051B	*Acheloos River*
SX-DBI	18355	051B	*Pinios River*
SX-DBK	18356	051B	*Strimon River*
SX-DBL	18420	051B	*Evros River*
SX-DBM	18687	051B	*Allakom River*
SX-DBN	18688	051B	*Hestos River*

Olympic's 720B fleet sits in storage at Athens in 1981. (Jon Proctor Collection)

Atlanta Skylarks

The Atlanta Skylarks travel club leased N7228U (msn 18081) from Independent Air, beginning in July 1973. The 720 was sub-leased several times before being sold in 1984.
Above: The 720-022 was photographed at Atlanta in January 1974, still wearing basic United colors. Notice the "mast-and-wire" antenna, unusual for a commercial jetliner. (Bruce Drum)
Below: Full Atlanta Skylarks titles appear on a slightly updated livery, seen at Reno in August 1981.
(Bob Van Hemert photo/Thomas Livesey Collection)

Atlanta Skylark's second 720 (msn 18159) was also leased from Independent Air. It retained the basic livery of earlier owner CONAIR and was issued American registration N7229L when Skylark took possession of the 720-025 on August 1, 1981. The final owner, Continental Aviation of India, purchased the aircraft in 1991 and transferred it to Nagpur, India. It remains stored in poor condition. (Stefano Pagiola Collection)

Dallas-based Club America sub-leased 720-025 N8711E (msn 18240) from Aero American Corporation in October 1973 for six months. Following this tour, the airplane migrated to Ambassadair. (Erik Bernhard Collection)

Wearing the simple red and white of the University of Nebraska's beloved "Cornhusker" football team, the Cornhusker Air Travel Club leased former United 720-022 N7218U (msn 18050) from My Seven Children, Inc. It is shown here in November 1974 at San Francisco International, just days after the aircraft was received. (Harry Sievers)

Fiesta Travel Club adopted previous operator Inair Panama's markings during its lease of the former United 720-022 N7226U (msn 18080) that commenced in October 1977. Seen at Phoenix, it wears registration N62215. (Erik Bernhard Collection)

Caesar's Chariot

Actually owned by Desert Palace, Inc., 720-022 N7224U (msn 18077) was recognized by its striking livery and Caesars Chariot titles. As a luxurious VIP aircraft, it flew high rollers to gambling casinos. The 720-022 bears small McCulloch titles by the forward boarding door, although the sub-lease to that company had already been completed when this picture was taken at Miami in December 1976. (Bruce Drum)

The Chariot received Led Zeppelin titles and tail markings during the band's 1977 tour. It was photographed during a stopover at New York-JFK. (Erik Bernhard Collection)

Sinclare Air Service purchased N7224U in August 1978 and made it available for films and concert tours. The Bee Gees used the handsomely painted aircraft for their "Spirits Having Flown" tour. In this picture taken at Miami in August 1979, the band's logo appears on the forward fuselage along with an image of the three Gibb brothers on the vertical fin. (Bruce Drum)

N7224U's black crown skin and tail finish was replaced with white paint and counterfeit Air France titles for a cameo appearance in a motion picture. The 720 was sold in 1987 to the Boeing Military Aircraft Company and broken up. (Jim Thompson Collection)

Contemporary Entertainment

Formed by entrepreneur Ward Sylvester Jr., Contemporary Entertainment Services, Inc. purchased the first 720 built from United Air Lines in January 1973 for $1 million, then spent a like amount fitting the interior with an opulent, 40-seat layout designed to attract traveling members of the entertainment industry. Christened *Starship I*, N7201U (msn 17907) brought upwards of $5 per mile in charter revenue. It would later wind up in the hands of Aeroamerica and finally be broken up in the United Kingdom at Luton Airport in 1982.

Starship I pauses during its Elton John tour charter in 1973, wearing maroon and gold. (Erik Bernhard Collection)

Obviously pleased with the product, the Elton John group chartered N7201U again in 1974. By then, *Starship I* had taken on an even more eye-catching livery. (Erik Bernhard Collection)

Horizons Travel Club sub-leased 720-022 N7228U (msn 18081) from Atlanta Skylarks from August 1983 until May 1984, applying only minimal refinements to its existing color scheme. (Erik Bernhard Collection)

Jet Set Travel Club of Bellevue, Washington utilized N7225U (msn 18078) for nearly 10 years. The yellow-and-blue livery remained on this 720-022 until it was broken up for spares at Kinshasa in 1989. (Jim Thompson Collection)

The Los Angeles Dodgers baseball club acquired N7536A (msn 18022) from American Airlines in January 1971 for $3 million plus the team's Lockheed 188 Electra. American re-configured the aircraft interior with four lounge-seating clusters as part of its 70-passenger layout. Re-registered N1R and named *Kay O' II* (after club owner Walter O'Mally's wife, Kay), the 720B transported the Dodgers for 12 seasons. It was sold to Great American Airways in 1983 but never placed into service. The Boeing Military Airplane Company subsequently bought N1R for use in the KC-135 spares program. (Harry Sievers)

The only turbofan-powered 720 operated by McCulloch was N7542A, leased from American Airlines for one year beginning in June 1972. It was photographed at Tulsa in full company colors. (Ted J. Gibson)

McCulloch		
Registration	msn	Model
N7201U	17907	022
N7207U	17913	022
N7542A	18028	023B
N7219U	18072	022
N7224U	18077	022

McCulloch International

Although technically an airline of sorts, McCulloch Properties actually organized its Long Beach, California-based air charter division in mid-1969 for the purpose of bringing potential buyers to see its various land development sites in Arizona, Nevada, Colorado and Arkansas. The operation began under the defunct Vance International Airlines certificate with Lockheed 188 Electra turboprops at the end of 1971. Boeing 720-023B N7542A was acquired for one year beginning in June 1972. Four non-fan 720s came and went during the next few years as well. Records indicated that only one, msn 17913, was owned, for a one-year period; the rest were leased. The air charter division eventually added contract work with NASA and the U.S. Navy, athletic and entertainment group charters. McCulloch International ceased operations in 1979.

McCulloch apparently operated some military charters with N7207U, as evidenced by this photo, taken at an unknown location. Bought from United in 1976, the 720-022 was sold only one year later. (Thomas Kim Collection)

Still owned by American Airlines and wearing its original registration number, N7529A's sale may have fallen through, as evidenced by this non-standard livery. The 720-023B sat in storage for more than three years before migrating to Somali Airlines. (via Nicky Scherrer)

In 1970, air travel club Voyager 1000 purchased former Eastern 720-022 N8702E (msn 18156) from Boeing for $1.6 million. N10VG was christened *Miss Indiana* and accommodated 155 passengers in its high-density configuration. The aircraft carried Boeing 707/720 titles during five years of service with Voyager. Acquired by Ambassadair in 1978, it was broken up at Miami in 1980. Voyager also operated a second 720-025, N15VG (msn 18163). (The Boeing Company Archives)

Windwalkers

Formally known as Windwalkers Air Country Club, the Columbus, Ohio-based travel group had 720-025 N8711E (msn 18240) painted up in this attractive livery with a cheatline curiously resembling that of Delta Air Lines. It was captured on film at Fort Lauderdale, Florida, wearing the name *Windwalker I* under the cockpit windows. N8711E was acquired in January 1983 and leased to another company in November 1984. (Nigel P. Chalcraft)

N7228U (msn 18081) was sub-leased by Windwalkers from Atlanta Skylarks in May 1984 and chartered by presidential contender Gary Hart. Following an engine fire on takeoff at Philadelphia in June, the 720-022 was ferried back to Columbus and withdrawn from use. This incident prompted an admonishment of Windwalkers from the government for operating a charter outside of the club's authority. The aircraft remained parked until owner Independent Air sold it for use as an anti-hijack trainer in Asia. Stripped of its titles, N7228U sits in the snow at Columbus shortly before its departure from the United States in December 1984. (Jim Thompson)

Government & Private Owners

Western Airlines sold N93145 (msn 18451) to Saudi Prince Nawab Bin Abdulaziz in 1978, and it was appropriately registered HZ-NAA. Sheik Kamal Adham obtained the aircraft in 1980 and applied HZ-KA1 to the 720-047B. Shown here in January 1982, the aircraft was painted in a two-tone blue and gold livery with a small Saudi Arabian flag on the forward fuselage. (Bryant Petitt Jr. Collection)

Sheik Adham had HZ-KA1 modified with hush-kits in 1987. Sold a year later, the aircraft has since been owned by JAR Aircraft Service.
Above: Photographed at Nice, France in October 1998, N720JR appears in this attractive livery with the JAR logo on the tail. (Denis Ciaudo)
Below: The same aircraft wears Republique du Congo titles in a September 1999 picture. (AviationTrade)

N92GS (msn 18452), originally N93146 with Western Airlines, was converted to an executive configuration in 1982. It changed hands several times before being purchased for scrap by Blue Metals, Inc. in 1992. The 720-047B was completely broken up in 1997. (via Nicky Scherrer)

Clad in an elegant livery of gold, white and green, the VIP 720-047B (HK-KA4, msn 18453) of Sheik Kamal Adham arrives at Washington-Dulles in 1978. Formerly N93147 with Western, the aircraft received a hush-kit modification in 1989. (R.J. Hurley)

The first 720-051 to enter service with Northwest Orient, N721US (msn 18351) was later modified to carry the president of Taiwan. Seen shortly before delivery, it still carries an American registration. The serial number 18351, which would become its new military registration, is taped over on the tail. Delivered on December 5, 1971, the aircraft remained in service until February 1996, when it was donated to the Republic of China Air Force Museum at Kangshan. (Harry Sievers Collection)

The 154th and final Boeing 720 produced, N3167 (msn 19523) spent 12 years with Western Airlines. The Government of Togo acquired the 720-047B in October 1980 and applied registration 5V-TAD. After only 36 months, it was sold to Boeing for use in the KC-135 spares program. (Thomas Livesey Collection)

Leased and later purchased from American Airlines, 720-023B A6-HHR (msn 18016) was used by the Dubai Air Wing from October 1975 to March 1982. It was then transferred to the Abu Dhabi Government for less than four months before being donated to Alyemda. (Terry Waddington Collection)

Spared from the cutter's torch, N64696 (msn 18073) has been retained by the George T. Baker Aviation School of Miami for use as a ground trainer. The rare, turbine-powered 720-022 remains intact and in good condition. (via Eddy Gual)

Test Beds

A five-engine 720B. The Allied Signal Aerospace flying test bed N720GT (msn 18384) is shown on final approach. A TFE731-60 turbofan engine is mounted to the starboard side of the fuselage, just aft of the cockpit. (Bob Trader photo/Phil Brooks Collection)

Honeywell International

The Garrett Engine Division of Allied Signal Aerospace acquired 720-051B N720GT from Conair in November 1987 for use as an engine and systems test bed. Based at Phoenix Sky Harbor International Airport, the aircraft most recently has been utilized for certification of the 7,000-pound-thrust AS900 family of turbofan engines.

Allied Signal acquired Honeywell in December 1999, changing its name to Honeywell International. Its 720B is based at Phoenix Sky Harbor International Airport, close to Honeywell facilities in Phoenix and Tempe.

Big Bird II, as identified by the name on the ventral fin, provides real-world operating conditions for the test engines. It is seen between flights at its Phoenix home base. (via Eddy Gual)

The 720B was updated in late 1999 with a new data acquisition system and adjustable-pitch, test-engine pylon capable of accommodating engines of up to 12,000 pounds thrust. In early 2000, a fresh livery was applied, along with the new registration N720H. Its modified pressurization system allows the aircraft to reach altititudes in excess of 45,000 feet. (Bob Shane)

Boeing repurchased this 720-051B (msn 18793) in June 1988 from its last airline customer, CONAIR, for $1.3 million, and spent another $2 million to transform it into a flying laboratory. Re-registered N771BE, the aircraft took to the air again in January 1989 to begin a variety of test programs including missile warning systems, high-accuracy direction finding, electronic warfare decoys and other defense and intelligence concepts. The cabin was reconfigured to house test equipment and up to 25 engineers, plus an air crew of four. Forty-two-inch wingtip extensions were added and the ventral fin was cut to accommodate a towed electronic warfare decoy, nicknamed "Big Boy." After completion of the test program in 1992, the aircraft was broken up at Paine Field, Washington. (The Boeing Company Archives)

Boeing also used this 720-025 (msn 18158), repossessed from Trans Polar, as a military projects test bed. It was equipped with Anti-Submarine Warfare (ASW) systems for projects conducted from 1972 through 1979. Pictured on the ramp at Boeing Field, Seattle, the aircraft retained much of the Trans Polar livery. The N3183B registration was later changed to N40102. It was parted out at Kingman, Arizona, starting in 1981. (J.A. Morrow photo/Terry Waddington Collection)

Hughes Aircraft bought ex-Ethiopian 720-060B ET-ABP (msn 18977) in 1989 for a platform to test the Advanced Infrared Measurements System (AIRMS). The port-side opening allowed the infrared sensor to look out of the aircraft through non-turbulent air. This "window" was part of an unpressurized enclosure for the sensor that was built into the fuselage, just forward of the wing. Aft of this section, a pressurized passenger compartment with 13 racks of electronics and three operator consoles supported the data collection. First registered N440DS, then N7381, the aircraft was turned over to the U.S. Air Force and served as part of an Advanced Research Projects Agency (ARPA)-sponsored effort, flying from Edwards Air Force Base and Mojave, both in California. *Embraceable Annie* is shown stored at Mojave, California, where it still resides, now the property of Aviation Warehouse. (Nicholas A. Veronico)

After hitting the cutters at a right angle, the 720 burst into flames as the number 3 engine exploded.

The right wing can be seen breaking away from the fuselage, now fully engulfed. The aircraft nose skids down the runway at a 90-degree angle.

The 720's nose is barely visible as the aircraft slides to a stop. Within 10 seconds, the fireball subsided, but residual burning continued around the jet for nearly two hours.

The charred fuselage of N833NA is examined by FAA and NASA investigators.

Hull Loses

Date	msn	Registration	Model	Operator	Location	Comments
12/04/61	18058	D-ABOK	030B	Lufthansa	Ebersheim, Germany	Training Flight; cause unknown
02/12/63	18354	N724US	051B	Northwest	Everglades, Florida	Structural failure
07/15/64	18249	D-ABOP	030B	Lufthansa	Ansbach, Germany	Training flight; structural failure
05/20/65	18379	AP-AMH	040B	PIA	Cairo, Egypt	On approach
01/09/68	18454	ET-AAG	060B	MEA	Beirut, Lebanon	DBR On landing
03/31/71	19439	N3166	047B	Western	Ontario, California	Training flight; on approach
09/13/74	18243	OY-DSR	025	CONAIR	Copenhagen, Denmark	DBR On landing
01/01/76	18020	OD-AFT	023B	MEA	Al Qaysumah, Saudi Arabia	Bomb; in flight
04/22/76	18044	N37777	022	US Global	Barranquilla, Colombia	On approach
06/27/76	18963	OD-AGE	047B	MEA	Beirut, Lebanon	Airport shelling
08/16/76	18831	HK-722	047B	AVIANCA	Mexico City, Mexico	DBR On landing
01/27/80	18087	HK-725	059B	AVIANCA	Quito, Ecuador	DBR On landing
01/08/81	18590	AP-AXK	047B	PIA	Quetta, Pakistan	DBR On landing
08/31/81	18018	OD-AFR	023B	MEA	Beirut, Lebanon	Bomb; on ground
06/12/82	18017	OD-AFP	023B	MEA	Beirut, Lebanon	Airport shelling
06/16/82	18029	OD-AFU	023B	MEA	Beirut, Lebanon	Airport shelling
06/16/82	18026	OD-AFW	023B	MEA	Beirut, Lebanon	Airport shelling
06/16/82	19161	OD-AGR	047B	MEA	Beirut, Lebanon	Airport shelling
08/01/82	18828	OD-AGG	047B	MEA	Beirut, Lebanon	Airport shelling
06/01/83	18035	OD-AFO	023B	MEA	Beirut, Lebanon	DBR Airport shelling
12/01/84	18066	N833NA	027	NASA	Edwards AFB, California	Controlled impact demonstration
08/21/85	18034	OD-AFL	023B	MEA	Beirut, Lebanon	Airport shelling
08/21/85	19160	OD-AGQ	047B	MEA	Beirut, Lebanon	Airport shelling

(DBR indicates damaged beyond economical repair)

Boeing 720-022 N7219U (msn 18072) is seen after it ran off the runway at Kansas City, Missouri in December 1977. The aircraft carried McCulloch International logos but had been returned to its lessor the previous March. Damage was minor, and the aircraft returned to service following repairs. (Jim Thompson Collection)

Appendix I
AIRCRAFT OPERATORS

The following list of 720 operators is in alphabetical order, with individual aircraft identified by the manufacturer's serial number (msn). This table provides a complete accounting of the initial and secondary operators of the 720, rather than the banks or finance companies that actually owned the aircraft. Several major carriers used 720s seasonally to assist with heavy traffic volumes. In addition, Some of these "operators" may not have actually flown the aircraft, using them instead as test platforms or cabin trainers. Due to space limitations, the companies that acquired 720s for the sole purpose of ferrying the aircraft to storage and subsequent dismantling have not been listed.

Aircraft Operator	msn	Aircraft Operator	msn
Abu Dhabi Government	18016	Belize Airways	17917, 18045, 18046,
Adham, Kamal (Sheik)	18451, 18453		18073, 18074, 18076
Aer Lingus	18041, 18042, 18043,	Bergin Avi Turkey	18060
	18820	Blue Metals	18452
Aeroamerica	17907, 17913, 18041,	Boeing	18158, 18793
	18042, 18064, 18065,	Braniff International Airways	18041-18043, 18064,
	18072, 18154, 18377,		18065, 18077, 18154,
	18423, 18581		18423, 18581
Aerocondor Colombia	18023, 18028	Britannia Airways	18163, 18820
Aeromar International	17915, 18072	British West Indian Airways	18043
Aeronaves Borinquena	18049	Caesars Chariot	18077
AERONICA –		Calair	18162, 18163, 18240,
Aerolineas Nicaraguenses	18688		18242, 18244
Aero Specialties Company	18048	Caledonian Airlines	18080
Aerotal – Aerolineas		Cavanagh Community	17915
Territoriales de Colombia	18060	Central Airlines	18425
Aero Tours Dominicana	18240	Club America	18240
Aerovias Quisqueyana	17913	Club International	18041, 18064, 18154,
Agro Air International	17915, 18072		18423
Air Bali	18080	CONAIR of Scandinavia	18157, 18159, 18161,
Air Cambodge	18043		18241, 18243, 18384,
Air Ceylon	18013, 18073		18421, 18422, 18792,
Air Charter Service	18078, 18162, 18244		18793
Air Cruise	18077	Congo Government	18451
Airfast	18043	Contemporary Entertainment	17907
Airline Training Institute	18064	Continental Airlines	18416-18419, 18587,
Air Malta	18063, 18167, 18378,		18763, 19002, 19003
	18380, 18793, 18820,	Continental Aviation Company	18159
	18827, 18829	Cornhusker Air Travel Club	18050
Air Niugini	18014	Cyprus Airways	18013, 18014
Air Rhodesia	18162, 18242, 18244	Cyprus Turkish Airlines (KTHY)	18423, 18581
Air Tanzania	18080, 18688	Dallah-Avco	18077
Air Viking	18075,18082, 18163	Delta Air Transport	18073
Air Zimbabwe	18162, 18242, 18244	Desert Palace	18077
Alaska Airlines	18042, 18049, 18376,	DETA Mozambique	18013
	18377, 18416	Dubai Government	18016
Alia – Royal Jordanian Airlines	18250, 18251	Eagle Air	18075, 18082, 18163,
Allied Signal	18384		18820, 18827
Alyemda	18016, 18032	Eastern Air Lines	18155-18164, 18240-18244
Ambassadair	18043, 18240	Eastern Orient Airlines	18423
Ambassador International	18423	Ecuatoriana	18033, 18036, 18037
American Airlines	18013-18037	EgyptAir	18423
American Trans Air	18043, 18156, 18240	El Al Israel Airlines	18041, 18043, 18424,
American Travel Air	18043		18425
Ariana Afghan Airlines	18060	Emerald Shillelagh	18043
Atlanta Skylarks	18081, 18159	Ethiopian Airlines	18417-18419,18454,
AVIANCA – Colombia	18057, 18059, 18061,		18455, 18977
	18086, 18087, 18248,	Faucett	18049
	18831	Famco Transport	18078
AVIATECA – Guatemala	18049, 18050, 18820	Federal Aviation Agency	18066

Aircraft Operator	msn	Aircraft Operator	msn
Fiesta Air Travel	18080	Panama National Airlines	18080
Floyd, Pearson, Richman & Greer	18452	Pan American World Airways	18033, 18036, 18037, 18042, 18049, 18057, 18059, 18060, 18248, 18250, 18251, 18376, 18377
Fontshi Aviation Service	18043		
Garuda Indonesian Airways	18381, 18383		
George T. Baker Aviation School	18073		
Global International Airways	18050, 18425		
Great American Airways	18022	Pan Aviation	18452
Gulf Air	18828	Pion Air	18048
Gulf Miles Company	18044	Pioneer International	18041
Hanna Industries	18041	Pratt & Whitney Canada	18021, 18024, 18027
Hispaniola Airways	18049	Private Jet Services	17907
Honeywell International	18384	Prince Nawaf Bin Abdulaziz	18451
Horizon Travel Club	18081	Race Aviation	18829
Hughes Aircraft	18977	Reef Hotel	17915
Huns Air	18048	Royal Air Maroc	18014, 18382
Inair Panama	18044, 18073	SAM Colombia	18057, 18059, 18248
Independent Air	18081, 18159	Saudi Arabian Airlines	18018, 18064, 18165, 18166, 18417, 18581, 18830
Inter American Air Cargo	18073		
Invicta Airlines	18013, 18014		
Iraqi Airways	18381	Seven Brothers	18050
Jet Charter Service	18381-18383	Sierra Leone Airlines	18251
Jet Set Travel Club	18078	Sierra Services	18078
Kenya Airways	18588, 18820	Silver Wings	18831
Korean Air Lines	18160, 18164	Sinclare Air Service	18077
Lambda Air	18072	Somali Airlines	18013, 18015, 18031
Led Zeppelin	18077	Southeast Airlines	18049
Libyan Arab Airlines	18026, 18049	Sudan Airways	18064, 18154, 18581
Los Angeles Dodgers Baseball Club	18022	Taiwan Government	18351
		Ten Miles High	18019
Lufthansa German Airlines	18057-18060, 18248-18251	360 Corporation	18077
Maersk Air	18384, 18421, 18422, 18792, 18793	TL Industries	18072
		Togo Government	19523
Maof Airlines	18013, 18014	Trans Caribbean Airways	18043
Marine, Inc.	18073	Trans European Airways	18043, 18155, 18384
McCulloch International Airlines	17907, 17913, 18028, 18072, 18077	Trans Polar Airlines	18041, 18043, 18158
		Trans World Airlines	18381-18384
Middle East Airlines	18017-18021, 18024-18027, 18029, 18030, 18034, 18035, 18454, 18455, 18828, 18830, 18963, 18977, 19160, 19161	Tropic Air	18049
		Tropicana	18581
		Tunis Air	18043, 18422, 18792
		United Air Lines	17907-17917, 18044-18050, 18072-18082
Monarch Airlines	18013, 18014, 18381, 18382, 18383, 18421, 18792	United States Air Force	18424, 18977
		Universal Airways	18080
My Seven Children	18050	Universal Applicators	18080
NASA	18031, 18066	US Global of Florida	18044, 18080
New ACS	18162	Voyager 1000	18156, 18163
Nigeria Airways	18026, 18384, 18422, 18793	West African Ventures	18044
		Western Airlines	18042, 18061-18063, 18167, 18376, 18377, 18451-18453, 18588-18590, 18749, 18818, 18820, 18827-18830, 18963, 19160, 19161, 19207, 19208, 19413, 19414, 19438, 19439, 19523
Northwest Orient Airlines	18351-18356, 18381-18384, 18420-18422, 18687, 18688, 18792, 18793		
Olympic Airways	18352, 18353, 18355, 18356, 18420, 18687, 18688		
		West Winds International Airlines	18077
Pacific Northern Airlines	18042, 18376, 18377	Windwalkers Air Country Club	18081, 18240
Pakistan International Airlines	18043, 18062, 18250, 18378-18380, 18581, 18589, 18590, 18745, 18749, 18818	Yemen Airways	18827
Pan African Express	18078		

Appendix II
REGISTRATION INDEX

Registration	msn	LN
A6 - UNITED ARAB EMIRATES		
A6-HHR	18016	150
AP - PAKISTAN		
AP-AMG	18378	257
AP-AMH	18379	321
AP-AMJ	18380	324
AP-ATQ	18745	380
AP-AXK	18590	339
AP-AXL	18818	390
AP-AXM	18749	374
AP-AXQ	18062	204
AP-AZP	18250	263
AP-BAF	18589	338
B - CHINA (REPUBLIC OF)		
18351	18351	211
C - CANADA		
C-FETB	18024	177
C-FWXI	18021	173
C-FWXL	18027	189
C9 - MOZAMBIQUE		
C9-ARG	18013	120
CX - URUGUAY		
CX-BQG	18829	427
D - GERMANY		
D-ABOH	18057	190
D-ABOK	18058	202
D-ABOL	18059	203
D-ABOM	18060	210
D-ABON	18248	258
D-ABOP	18249	262
D-ABOQ	18250	263
D-ABOR	18251	273
D-ACIP	18162	240
D-ACIQ	18163	241
D-ACIR	18240	246
D-ACIS	18242	248
D-ACIT	18244	255
EI - EIRE (IRELAND)		
EI-ALA	18041	172
EI-ALB	18042	182
EI-ALC	18043	188
EL - LIBERIA		
EL-AKD	18030	195
ET - ETHIOPIA		
ET-AAG	18165	250
ET-AAG	18454	319
ET-AAH	18166	251
ET-AAH	18455	322
ET-ABP	18977	442
ET-AFA	18418	300

Registration	msn	LN
ET-AFB	18419	304
ET-AFK	18417	295
G - GREAT BRITAIN		
G-AZFB	18381	222
G-AZKM	18382	223
G-AZNX	18383	230
G-BBZG	18792	381
G-BCBA	18014	143
G-BCBB	18013	120
G-BHGE	18421	244
G-BRDR	18688	361
HC - ECUADOR		
HC-AZO	18033	206
HC-AZP	18036	215
HC-AZQ	18037	220
HC-BDP	18033	206
HI - DOMINICAN REPUBLIC		
HI-372	17915	146
HI-401	18049	186
HI-415	18072	252
HK - COLOMBIA		
HK-1973	18023	166
HK-1974	18028	193
HK-1974X	18028	193
HK-2558	18060	210
HK-2558X	18060	210
HK-676	18059	203
HK-677	18057	190
HK-723	18061	197
HK-724	18086	245
HK-725	18087	249
HK-726	18831	414
HK-749	18248	258
HL - REPUBLIC OF KOREA		
HL-7402	18160	236
HL-7403	18164	242
HP - PANAMA		
HP-679	18080	284
HP-685	18044	178
HZ - SAUDI ARABIA		
HZ-ACA	18165	250
HZ-ACB	18166	251
HZ-KA1	18451	307
HZ-KA4	18453	314
HZ-NAA	18451	307
JY - JORDAN		
JY-ADS	18250	263
JY-ADT	18251	273
LN - NORWAY		
LN-TUU	18041	172

Registration	msn	LN
LN-TUV	18043	188
LN-TUW	18158	234
N - UNITED STATES OF AMERICA		
N10VG	18156	232
N110DS	18063	213
N113	18066	208
N15VG	18163	241
N17207	19002	473
N17208	19003	474
N1776Q	18041	172
N18KM	18019	158
N1R	18022	174
N210DS	18167	221
N2143J	18451	307
N23	18066	208
N2464C	18381	222
N2464K	18382	223
N24666	18383	230
N2628Y	18165	250
N2697V	18066	208
N28JS	18044	178
N301AS	18376	279
N302AS	18377	285
N303AS	18042	182
N304AS	18049	186
N3124Z	18157	233
N3154	18827	410
N3155	18828	423
N3156	18829	427
N3157	18830	429
N3158	18963	433
N3159	19160	470
N3160	19161	481
N3161	19207	512
N3162	19208	514
N3163	19413	581
N3164	19414	597
N3165	19438	615
N3166	19439	621
N3167	19523	624
N3183B	18158	234
N321E	18423	289
N330DS	18455	322
N341A	18014	143
N3746E	18060	210
N37777	18044	178
N3831X	18059	203
N3833L	19523	624
N40102	18158	234
N417MA	18082	298
N419MA	18082	298
N421MA	18049	186
N4228G	18425	290
N440DS	18977	442

Registration	msn	LN	Registration	msn	LN	Registration	msn	LN
N4450Z	18831	414	N7228U	18081	297	N785PA	18060	210
N4451B	18086	245	N7229L	18159	235	N786PA	18248	258
N5487N	18380	324	N7229U	18082	298	N787PA	18250	263
N550DS	18417	295	N722US	18352	218	N788PA	18251	273
N57201	18416	288	N723US	18353	219	N791TW	18381	222
N57202	18417	295	N724US	18354	224	N792TW	18382	223
N57203	18418	300	N725US	18355	231	N793TW	18383	230
N57204	18419	304	N726US	18356	238	N795TW	18384	237
N57205	18587	340	N727US	18420	243	N8215Q	18688	361
N57206	18763	382	N728US	18421	244	N833NA	18066	208
N62215	18080	284	N729US	18422	256	N8498S	18424	281
N64696	18073	253	N730T	18154	226	N8498T	18425	290
N68646	18745	380	N730US	18381	222	N8701E	18155	225
N7076	18064	187	N731T	18423	289	N8702E	18156	232
N7077	18065	196	N731US	18382	223	N8703E	18157	233
N7078	18066	208	N732US	18383	230	N8704E	18158	234
N7078	18154	226	N733T	18581	347	N8705E	18159	235
N7079	18423	289	N733US	18384	237	N8706E	18160	236
N7080	18581	347	N734T	18041	172	N8707E	18161	239
N7081	18042	182	N734T	18065	196	N8708E	18162	240
N7082	18043	188	N734US	18687	351	N8709E	18163	241
N7083	18041	172	N735US	18688	361	N8710E	18164	242
N7201U	17907	085	N736T	18064	187	N8711E	18240	246
N7202U	17908	095	N736US	18792	381	N8712E	18241	247
N7203U	17909	109	N737US	18793	384	N8713E	18242	248
N7204U	17910	130	N7381	18977	442	N8714E	18243	254
N7205U	17911	131	N7527A	18013	120	N8715E	18244	255
N7206U	17912	132	N7528A	18014	143	N8790R	18043	188
N7207U	17913	141	N7529A	18015	149	N92GS	18452	310
N7208U	17914	142	N7530A	18016	150	N93136	18165	250
N7209U	17915	146	N7531A	18017	156	N93137	18250	263
N720AC	18016	150	N7532A	18018	157	N93141	18061	197
N720BC	18251	273	N7533A	18019	158	N93142	18062	204
N720BG	18033	206	N7534A	18020	165	N93143	18063	213
N720CC	17915	146	N7535A	18021	173	N93144	18167	221
N720GT	18384	237	N7536A	18022	174	N93145	18451	307
N720H	18384	237	N7537A	18023	166	N93146	18452	310
N720PW	18021	173	N7538A	18024	177	N93147	18453	314
N720JR	18451	307	N7539A	18025	180	N93148	18588	337
N720V	18376	279	N7540A	18026	181	N93149	18589	338
N720W	18377	285	N7541A	18027	189	N93150	18590	339
N7210U	17916	147	N7542A	18028	193	N93151	18749	374
N7211U	17917	148	N7543A	18029	194	N93152	18818	390
N7212U	18044	178	N7544A	18030	195	N93153	18820	401
N7213U	18045	179	N7545A	18031	198			
N7214U	18046	183	N7546A	18032	199	**OD - LEBANON**		
N7215U	18047	184	N7547A	18033	206	OD-AFL	18034	207
N7216U	18048	185	N7548A	18034	207	OD-AFM	18027	189
N7217U	18049	186	N7549A	18035	214	OD-AFN	18030	195
N7218U	18050	191	N7550A	18036	215	OD-AFO	18035	214
N7219U	18072	252	N7551A	18037	220	OD-AFP	18017	156
N721US	18351	211	N769BE	18418	300	OD-AFQ	18024	177
N7220U	18073	253	N770BE	18419	304	OD-AFR	18018	157
N7221U	18074	259	N771BE	18793	384	OD-AFS	18019	158
N7222U	18075	260	N780EC	18033	206	OD-AFT	18020	165
N7223U	18076	261	N780PA	18033	206	OD-AFU	18029	194
N7224U	18077	265	N781PA	18036	215	OD-AFW	18026	181
N7225U	18078	267	N782PA	18037	220	OD-AFZ	18025	180
N7226U	18079	278	N783PA	18057	190	OD-AGB	18021	173
N7227U	18080	284	N784PA	18059	203	OD-AGE	18963	433
						OD-AGF	18830	429

Registration	msn	LN	Registration	msn	LN	Registration	msn	LN
OD-AGG	18828	423	TF-VLA	18163	241	4X-BMB	18013	120
OD-AGQ	19160	470	TF-VLB	18827	410	4X-JYG	18013	120
OD-AGR	19161	481	TF-VLC	18820	401			
			TF-VVA	18082	298	**5V - TOGO**		
OO - BELGIUM			TF-VVB	18075	260	5V-TAD	19523	624
OO-TEA	18155	225	TF-VVE	18163	241			
OO-TEB	18043	188				**5Y - KENYA**		
OO-TYA	18384	237	**VP-H - BELIZE**			5Y-BBX	18588	337
OO-VGM	18073	253	VP-HCM	18046	183			
			VP-HCN	18074	259	**6O - SOMALIA**		
OY - DENMARK			VP-HCO	18045	179	6O-SAX	18031	198
			VP-HCP	17917	148	6O-SAU	18013	120
OY-APU	18792	381	VP-HCQ	18076	261	6O-SAW	18015	149
OY-APV	18793	384						
OY-APW	18422	256	**VP-Y - RHODESIA**			**7O - YEMEN**		
OY-APY	18421	244	VP-YNL	18162	240	7O-ABQ	18032	199
OY-APZ	18384	237	VP-YNM	18242	248	7O-ACP	18016	150
OY-DSK	18157	233	VP-YNN	18244	255			
OY-DSL	18159	235				**9H - MALTA**		
OY-DSM	18161	239	**VT - INDIA**			9H-AAK	18063	213
OY-DSP	18241	247	VT-ERS	18159	235	9H-AAL	18167	221
OY-DSR	18243	254				9H-AAM	18378	257
			XA - MEXICO			9H-AAN	18380	324
P2 - PAPUA NEW GUINEA			XA-SDL	18072	252	9H-AAO	18829	427
P2-ANG	18014	143						
			YA - AFGHANISTAN			**9L - SIERRA LEONE**		
SX - GREECE			YA-HBA	18060	210	9L-LAZ	18251	273
SX-DBG	18352	218						
SX-DBH	18353	219	**YN - NICARAGUA**			**9Q - ZAIRE**		
SX-DBI	18355	231	YN-BYI	18688	361	9Q-CFT	18043	188
SX-DBK	18356	238				9Q-CTD	18162	240
SX-DBL	18420	243	**Z - ZIMBABWE**			9Q-CTM	18078	267
SX-DBM	18687	351	Z-YNL	18162	240			
SX-DBN	18688	361	Z-YNN	18244	255	**9Y - TRINIDAD AND TOBAGO**		
						9Y-TCS	18043	188
TF - ICELAND			**4R - CEYLON (SRI LANKA)**					
TF-AYA	18792	381	4R-ACS	18013	120			
TF-AYB	18422	256						
TF-AYC	18421	244	**4X - ISRAEL**					
TF-AYD	18793	384	4X-ABA	18424	281			
			4X-ABB	18425	290			
			4X-BMA	18014	143			

Appendix III
PRODUCTION LIST

All 154 Boeing 720 and 720B aircraft are listed in order by the manufacturer's serial number (msn). The Line Number identifies the aircraft position in final assembly (the 707 and 720 Line Numbers shared a common list). The Model Number identifies the type of aircraft specific to the customer (the suffix "B" identifies the aircraft as having turbofan engines). The Block Number is used internally by Boeing for planning and is often visible as the aircraft makes its way through the assembly process. After delivery, an aircraft is identified by either its serial number or by its

Registration Number. The registration (tail) number may be changed but the serial number always remains with the aircraft. The information contained in the Current Status column provides the disposition of the aircraft as well as its location (if known). Two sets of abbreviations are used in this column. The first signifies the status of the aircraft. The second set lists abbreviations representing the location. The Last Known Operator column provides a listing of the most recent owner or lessor using the aircraft in commercial service, as well as the Registration Number of the aircraft at that time.

Current Status disposition codes:

BU	broken up
DIS	on display as a museum, restaurant or other non-flying use
IS	in service (HK signifies that the aircraft engines have been modified with hush kits)
WFU	withdrawn from use
WO	written off
WO ACC	written off - accident (see Chapter V for details)

Current Status location codes:

ADE	Aden, Yemen
AMARC	Aerospace Maintenance and Regeneration Center, Davis-Monthan AFB, AZ
ATH	Athens, Greece
BAQ	Barranquilla, Colombia
BEY	Beirut, Lebanon
BFI	Boeing Field, Seattle
BLL	Billund, Denmark
BOG	Bogota, Colombia
BOH	Bournemouth, U.K.
BOM	Bombay, India
CAI	Cairo, Egypt
CPH	Copenhagen, Denmark
DEN	Denver, Colorado
EAFB	Edwards AFB, California
FIH	Kinshasa, Congo
HKG	Hong Kong
HRE	Harare, Zimbabwe
IGM	Kingman, Arizona
KFK	Keflavik, Iceland
KHI	Karachi, Pakistan
LHE	Lahore, Pakistan
LTN	Luton, U.K.
MEX	Mexico City, Mexico
MGQ	Mogadishu, Somalia
MHV	Mojave, California
MIA	Miami, Florida
MJM	Mbuji-Mayi, Congo
MLA	Luqa, Malta
MSP	Minneapolis, Minnesota
MWH	Moses Lake, Washington
MZJ	Marana, Arizona
NAG	Nagpur, India
NBO	Nairobi, Kenya
PAI	Paine Field, Washington
PAP	Port-au-Prince, Haiti
PEK	Beijing, China
PHX	Phoenix, Arizona
PIE	St. Petersburg, Florida
POP	Puerta Plata, Dominican Republic
SEL	Seoul, South Korea
SNN	Shannon, Ireland
STN	London-Stansted, U.K.
THF	Berlin-Templehof, Germany
TLV	Tel Aviv, Israel
UET	Quetta, Pakistan
UIO	Quito, Ecuador
YHU	St-Hubert, P.Q., Canada

msn	Line Number	Model Number	Block Number	First Flight	Delivery Date	Initial Operator	Registration Number	Current Status	Last Known Operator (Registration Number)
18167	221	047B	B2204	07-03-61	08-15-61	Western	N93144	BU MZJ	Air Malta (9H-AAL)
18240	246	025	B0511	10-24-61	01-09-62	Eastern	N8711E	WFU PAP	Aerotours Dominicano (N8711E)
18241	247	025	B0512	10-30-61	11-13-61	Eastern	N8712E	DIS BLL	Conair of Scandinavia (OY-DSP)
18242	248	025	B0513	11-13-61	11-22-61	Eastern	N8713E	BU HRE	Air Zimbabwe (Z-YNM)
18243	254	025	B0514	12-01-61	12-08-61	Eastern	N8714E	BU CPH	Conair of Scandinavia (OY-DSR)
18244	255	025	B0515	12-07-61	12-10-61	Eastern	N8715E	BU HRE	Air Zimbabwe (Z-YNN)
18248	258	030B	B2005	12-20-61	01-05-62	Lufthansa	D-ABON	DIS BOG	SAM Colombia (HK-749)
18249	262	030B	B2006	01-04-62	01-12-62	Lufthansa	D-ABOP	WO ACC	Lufthansa (D-ABOP)
18250	263	030B	B2007	01-09-62	03-23-62	Lufthansa	D-ABOQ	DIS KHI	Pakistan Intl (AP-AZP)
18251	273	030B	B2008	02-16-62	02-26-62	Lufthansa	D-ABOR	BU AMARC	Sierra Leone (9L-LAZ)
18351	211	051B	B2101	05-20-61	05-26-61	Northwest	N721US	MSM GSN	Rep. of China Air Force (18351)
18352	218	051B	B2102	06-09-61	07-23-61	Northwest	N722US	BU ATH	Olympic Airways (SX-DBG)
18353	219	051B	B2103	06-19-61	08-02-61	Northwest	N723US	BU ATH	Olympic Airways (SX-DBH)
18354	224	051B	B2106	07-14-61	08-24-61	Northwest	N724US	WO ACC	Northwest (N724US)
18355	231	051B	B2108	08-23-61	09-27-61	Northwest	N725US	BU SNN	Olympic Airways (SX-DBI)
18356	238	051B	B2110	09-21-61	10-05-61	Northwest	N726US	BU ATH	Olympic Airways (SX-DBK)
18376	279	062	B0401	02-16-62	03-23-62	Pacific Northern	N720V	BU MIA	Alaska Airlines (N301AS)
18377	285	062	B0402	04-09-62	04-18-62	Pacific Northern	N720W	BU THF	Alaska Airlines (N302AS)
18378	257	040B	B2114	12-12-61	12-21-61	Pakistan	AP-AMG	BU MLA	Air Malta (9H-AAM)
18379	321	040B	B2115	10-19-62	11-06-62	Pakistan	AP-AMH	WO CAI	Pakistan International (AP-AMH)
18380	324	040B	B2116	11-14-62	11-29-62	Pakistan	AP-AMJ	BU AMARC	Air Malta (9H-AAN)
18381	222	051B	B2104	07-14-61	08-09-61	Trans World	N791TW	BU AMARC	Jet Charter Service (N2464C)
18382	223	051B	B2105	06-25-61	08-17-61	Trans World	N792TW	BU AMARC	Jet Charter Service (N2464K)
18383	230	051B	B2107	08-11-61	09-19-61	Trans World	N793TW	BU AMARC	Jet Charter Service (N24666)
18384	237	051B	B2109	09-15-61	09-30-61	Trans World	N795TW	IS PHX	Allied Signal Aerospace (N720GT)
18416	288	024B	B2601	04-19-62	04-30-62	Continental	N57201	BU MIA	Continental (N57201)
18417	295	024B	B2602	05-18-62	05-27-62	Continental	N57202	BU AMARC	Ethiopian (ET-AFK)
18418	300	024B	B2603	06-13-62	06-20-62	Continental	N57203	BU AMARC	Ethiopian (ET-AFA)
18419	304	024B	B2604	06-29-62	07-07-62	Continental	N57204	BU AMARC	Ethiopian (ET-AFB)
18420	243	051B	B2111	10-13-61	10-25-61	Northwest	N727US	BU ATH	Olympic Airways (SX-DBL)
18421	244	051B	B2112	10-04-61	11-14-61	Northwest	N728US	BU AMARC	CONAIR of Scandinavia (OY-APY)
18422	256	051B	B2113	12-05-61	12-13-61	Northwest	N729US	BU AMARC	CONAIR of Scandinavia (OY-APW)
18423	289	027	B0305	04-27-62	05-10-62	Braniff	N7079	BU BOH	Eastern Orient (N321E)
18424	281	058B	B2091	03-16-62	03-26-62	El Al	4X-ABA	BU AMARC	Jet Power (N8498S)
18425	290	058B	B0292	04-23-62	04-30-62	El Al	4X-ABB	BU AMARC	Jet Power (N4228G)
18451	307	047B	B2205	07-19-62	07-27-62	Western	N93145	IS (HK)	JAR Aircraft Service (N720JR)
18452	310	047B	B2206	07-13-62	08-08-62	Western	N93146	BU MIA	Pan Aviation (N92GS)
18453	314	047B	B2207	08-22-62	08-28-62	Western	N93147	IS (HK)	Sheik Kamal Adham (HZ-KA4)
18454	319	060B	B2551	10-04-62	11-02-62	Ethiopian	ET-AAG	WO BEY	MEA (ET-AAG)
18455	322	060B	B2552	11-01-62	11-27-62	Ethiopian	ET-AAH	BU AMARC	Ethiopian (ET-AAH)
18581	347	027	B0306	08-08-63	08-22-63	Braniff	N7080	BU BFI	Aeroamerica (N733T)

msn	Line Number	Model Number	Block Number	First Flight	Delivery Date	Initial Operator	Registration Number	Current Status	Last Known Operator (Registration Number)
18587	340	024B	B2605	05-03-63	05-11-63	Continental	N57205	BU MZJ	Continental (N57205)
18588	337	047B	B2208	03-21-63	04-03-63	Western	N93148	WFU NBO	Kenya Airways (5Y-BBX)
18589	338	047B	B2209	04-11-63	04-23-63	Western	N93149	BU KHI	Pakistan International (AP-BAF)
18590	339	047B	B2210	04-19-63	05-02-63	Western	N93150	BU UET	Pakistan International (AP-AXK)
18687	351	051B	B2191	09-24-63	10-22-63	Northwest	N734US	BU ATH	Olympic Airways (SX-DBM)
18688	361	051B	B2192	01-17-64	01-23-64	Northwest	N735US	BU AMARC	Aeronica (YN-BYI)
18745	380	040B	B2199	07-07-64	04-23-65	Pakistan	AP-ATQ	BU TLV	Pakistan International (AP-ATQ)
18749	374	047B	B2211	05-07-64	05-21-64	Western	N93151	DIS KHI	Pakistan International (AP-AXM)
18763	382	024B	B2606	07-05-64	07-15-64	Continental	N57206	BU MZJ	Continental (N57206)
18792	381	051B	B2193	06-18-64	06-18-64	Northwest	N736US	BU AMARC	CONAIR of Scandinavia (OY-APU)
18793	384	051B	B2194	07-21-64	07-21-64	Northwest	N737US	BU PAI	Boeing Equipment Hldg. (N771BE)
18818	390	047B	B2212	07-23-64	09-23-64	Western	N93152	BU LHE	Pakistan International (AP-AXL)
18820	401	047B	B2213	01-13-65	01-21-65	Western	N93153	BU STN	Eagle Air (TF-VLC)
18827	410	047B	B2214	02-01-65	03-09-65	Western	N3154	BU SNN	Eagle Air (TF-VLB)
18828	423	047B	B2215	05-10-65	05-19-65	Western	N3155	WO BEY	MEA (OD-AGG)
18829	427	047B	B2216	05-26-65	06-02-65	Western	N3156	BU AMARC	Air Malta (9H-AAO)
18830	429	047B	B2217	06-11-65	06-17-65	Western	N3157	WFU BEY	MEA (OD-AGF)
18831	414	059B	B2403	03-24-65	04-06-65	AVIANCA	HK-726	BU AMARC	Silver Wings (N4450Z)
18963	433	047B	B2218	07-18-65	07-21-65	Western	N3158	WO BEY	MEA (OD-AGE)
18977	442	060B	B2553	09-01-65	09-20-65	Ethiopian	ET-ABP	WFU MHV	Raytheon (N7381)
19002	473	024B	B2607	02-08-66	02-16-66	Continental	N17207	BU MZJ	Continental (N17207)
19003	474	024B	B2608	02-14-66	02-19-66	Continental	N17208	BU BFI	Continental (N17208)
19160	470	047B	B2219	01-20-66	01-29-66	Western	N3159	WO BEY	MEA (OD-AGQ)
19161	481	047B	B2220	03-04-66	03-12-66	Western	N3160	WO BEY	MEA (OD-AGR)
19207	512	047B	B2221	07-23-66	07-27-66	Western	N3161	BU AMARC	Western (N3161)
19208	514	047B	B2222	07-26-66	07-27-66	Western	N3162	BU AMARC	Western (N3162)
19413	581	047B	B2223	05-05-67	05-13-67	Western	N3163	BU AMARC	Western (N3163)
19414	597	047B	B2224	06-22-67	06-27-67	Western	N3164	BU AMARC	Western (N3164)
19438	615	047B	B2225	08-11-67	08-18-67	Western	N3165	BU AMARC	Western (N3165)
19439	621	047B	B2226	08-27-67	09-07-67	Western	N3166	WO ACC	Western (N3166)
19523	624	047B	B2227	09-08-67	09-20-67	Western	N3167	BU AMARC	Government of Togo (5V-TAD)

BIBLIOGRAPHY

Books

Bowers, Peter M. *Boeing Aircraft since 1916.* London: Putnam Books, 1989.

Cearley, Jr., George W. *Boeing 707 & 720.* Dallas, Texas: George W. Cearley Jr., 1993.

Davies, R.E.G. *Airlines of Latin America since 1919.* Washington, D.C.: Smithsonian Institution Press, 1984.

—. *Delta - An Airline and its Aircraft,* McLean, Virginia: Paladwr Press, 1990.

—. *Saudia: An Airline and its Aircraft.* McLean, Virginia: Paladwr Press, 1995.

Denham, Terry. *World Directory of Airliner Cashes.* Sparkford, U.K.: Patrick Stephens Limited, 1996.

Eastwood, A.B & Roach, J.R. *Jet Airliner Production List, Vol. I.* Middlesex, U.K.: The Aviation Hobby Shop, 1999.

Francillon, René. *Boeing 707 - Pioneer Jetliner.* Osceola, Wisconsin: MBI Publishing Co., 1999.

Gero, David. *Aviation Disasters.* Sparkford, U.K.: Patrick Stephens Limited, 1993.

Goldman, Marvin G. *El Al - Star in the Sky.* Miami, Florida: World Transport Press, 1990.

Hurturk, Kivanc N. *Individual Aircraft History of the Boeing 707.* Forest Hills, N.Y.: Buchair (USSA), Inc. 1998.

Job, Macarthur. *Air Disaster - Volume 1.* Weston Creek, Australia: Aerospace Publications Pty Ltd., 1994.

Klee, Ulrich. *JP Airline-Fleets* (various issues). Glattbrugg, Switzerland: Buchair & Co.

Lloyd, William M. & Nash, H.J.; Sievers, Harry; Whittle, John A. *The Boeing 707 and 720.* Peterborough, U.K.:
    Air Britain (Historians) Ltd., 1972.

Mills, Stephen E. *More than Meets the Sky.* Seattle, Washington: Superior Publishing Co., 1972.

Proctor, Jon. *Convair 880 & 990.* Miami, Florida: World Transport Press, 1996.

Rummel, Robert W. *Howard Hughes and TWA.* Washington, D.C.: Smithsonian Institution Press, 1991.

Satterfield, Archie. *The Alaska Airlines Story.* Anchorage, Alaska: Alaska Northwest Publishing Co., 1981.

Serling, Robert J. *Eagle – The Story of American Airlines.* New York, New York: St. Martins/Marek, 1985

—. *From the Captain to the Colonel – An Informal History of Eastern Airlines.* New York, New York: Dial Press, 1980.

—. *Howard Hughes' Airline – An Informal History of TWA.* New York, New York: St. Martins/Marek, 1983.

—. *Maverick – The Story of Robert Six and Continental Airlines.* Garden City, New York: Doubleday & Company, 1974.

—. *The Only Way to Fly — The Story of Western Airlines.* Garden City, New York: Doubleday & Company, 1976.

Periodicals

Airliner. Boeing Commercial Airplane Company (various issues).

Annual Report – Northwest Airlines (various issues).

Boeing News (various issues).

Flagship News. American Airlines (various issues)

New Highways in the Sky. Boeing Commercial Airplane Company, 1976.

TWA Skyliner. Trans World Airlines (various issues)

U.S. Standard Jet Transport Characteristics. The Boeing Company, 1991.

The following magazines and periodicals were sources of additional information:

Air Transport World; Airline Executive; Airliners Magazine; Aviation International News; Aviation-Letter; Aviation Week & Space Technology; Back Aviation Services/Lundkvist Fleet Database; Captain's Log (World Airline Historical Society); *Flight International; Official Airline Guide; The New York Times; St. Paul Pioneer Press; The Wall Street Journal; World Airline Fleets News*

Websites:

Aviation Safety Network: *http://aviation-safety.net/*

Commercial Jet Aircraft Census: *http://www.bird.ch/bharms/asr_sh00.htm*

Ethiopian Airlines: *http://www.ethiopian-airline.com/*

National Transportation Safety Board (NTSB): *http://www.ntsb.gov*

The Boeing Company Archives